FLY NAVY

The View from a 'Jungly' Cockpit 1958 - 2008

Collated by JOHN BEATTIE

Edited by RICK JOLLY

Illustrated by LEE HOWARD

Front Cover: *A painting by David Hardstaff of the rescue of two badly injured
survivors from HMS Ardent, by the crew of a passing Wessex HU.5 helicopter
of 845 Naval Air Squadron during the Battle of Falkland Sound, Friday May
21st 1982. This incident is described in more detail at pp 84-88.*

Page vi: *HRH The Prince of Wales in a Wessex HU.5 of Red Dragon Flight.
(© Tom Stoddard/Rex Features)*

Rear Cover: *A photo montage depicting a miscellany of Fleet Air Arm aircraft,
including (in alphabetical order): Albacore; Lynx (two versions); Osprey; Pup;
Sea Fury; Sea Hawk; Sea King; Sea Vixen; Swordfish; Wasp; Wessex;
Whirlwind.*

ACKNOWLEDGEMENTS

JB is very grateful to every individual who helped him in his research for articles to place in this book. He also wishes to thank everyone who penned their stories for him, although he feels that there are many good tales out there that are still to be told. You might hear one on a ski lift, or in a bar - or wherever Junglies choose to gather and reminisce. Please pause to record them - and then send them in!

Especial thanks go to the authors of three books who have willingly allowed him to use their work - firstly Rick Jolly OBE, for **'THE RED AND GREEN LIFE MACHINE'** - the story of the Falklands Field Hospital, available direct from the publishers at PO Box 42, Torpoint PL11 3EB, price £10 (which includes P&P). His royalties go to the charity **Combat Stress**.

Second, James Newton DFC for his superb account of Navy anti-tank helicopter ops during the Gulf campaign - **'ARMED ACTION'** (in hardback and paperback), available at all good booksellers (ISBN 978-0-7553-1601-4).

Thirdly, Dick Hutchings' excellent, hitherto secret story of an important aspect of the South Atlantic campaign - Special Forces operations behind the lines. **'SPECIAL FORCES PILOT'** comes from Pen & Sword Books at *www.pen-and-sword.co.uk* (ISBN 978-1-84415804 1).

My days spent as a Junglie pilot in the early nineteen seventies were undoubtedly some of the most enjoyable of my naval career. The flying was wonderfully varied, often demanding and always exhilarating, and the spirit among aircrew and maintainers was second to none.

I was privileged to join the Red Dragon Flight of 845 Squadron, comprising two finely tuned, very red Wessex Vs, with a dedicated and loyal band of maintainers. On embarking in H.M.S. HERMES, I was reassured to hear from Wings that nothing had been left to chance in order to ensure my wellbeing, so it was quite a surprise shortly afterwards to experience a dramatic engine failure en route to a rocket-firing sortie, requiring me to put down somewhat hastily in a North Somerset ploughed field (rather expertly, I thought!), much to the initial outrage and subsequent incredulity of the local farmer, who kindly said I could come back whenever I wished! I also soon learned that no amount of assurance could protect the Flight from Murphy's Law, as deftly proved one day by an aircraft handler as he proudly lowered the deck lift containing one of the Red Dragon aircraft – all except its main wheels which remained firmly secured to the flight deck. Sadly, I was not present to hear Wings' views on this incident, but I much enjoyed Tugg Wilson's take on it later!

Over the years, both in peacetime and in war, the Junglies have earned an enviable reputation for 'getting the job done'; a reputation as justified in the current theatres of conflict as it was during those early days in the jungles of Borneo. This has called for qualities which we readily associate with the Junglie: determination, resourcefulness, quick thinking and courage, all of which I witnessed in abundance during my time in 845. The other ubiquitous quality I greatly enjoyed was the Junglies' irrepressible sense of humour, examples of which are much in evidence in this book.

The book, I feel sure, only scratches the surface of the veritable mine of Junglie tales, some no doubt apochryphal, some very slightly embellished, but all definitely worthy of re-telling. I warmly commend it to you.

©**Tugg** and the Editor, *Navy News*

The Production Team

John Beattie cajoled, persuaded, gathered in, and then selected and assembled all the Jungly tales that make up this book. He was himself trained as a Jungly, serving with 846, 847, 848 and 707 Squadrons in turn, before becoming Senior Naval Officer at the Royal Norwegian Air Force Base in Bardufoss. In addition to his operational and intructuctional duties, he also flew aircraft of the RN Historic Flight from 1986 to 1994, before retiring to airline flying. After captaincy first on the *Dart Herald* and then on *BAe 146* jets, he returned to the RNHF as its civilian manager in 2004, at the age of 60. 'JB' is a lifelong aircraft enthusiast who owns his own *Chipmunk* trainer, and continues to fly airshow displays in privately-owned de Havilland *Venom*, Supermarine *Seafire* and Douglas *Skyraider* aircraft.

Rick Jolly is a retired Surgeon Captain RN who spent most of his 25 year career with the Royal Marines and Fleet Air Arm, gaining a green beret and the Diploma in Aviation Medicine along the way. His experience of active service in Northern Ireland and SAR flying at RNAS Culdrose combined to good effect in the Falklands War, when he commanded the British field hospital at Ajax Bay. Unusually, he was then decorated by both sides - the *OBE* from HM The Queen, and the *Order of May* from a democratic Argentine government when they later discovered his care for over 200 of their wounded. Every single casualty, of both sides, spent time in a Royal Navy (mainly Jungly) helicopter. He now works part-time for the MoD and writes articles and books about Naval and Tri-service humour, as well as cheerfully volunteering for the huge personal task of typesetting and proof-reading this book for its publication!

Lee Howard was trained as an aircraft engineer at RN Aircraft Yard Fleetlands, near Gosport, before moving on to a white-collar engineering job at RN Air Station Yeovilton in 2003. In addition to his daytime duties, he is a skilled and well-published aviation historian and photographer. Lee has co-authored several books about Naval aircraft, runs the RN Historic Flight website and has also designed two of the RNHF's publicity brochures. For this particular book he has trawled the archives, then carefully assembled a collection of Commando helicopter photos that represent 50 years of Jungly aviation.

The Royal Navy Historic Flight

The Royal Navy Historic Flight (RNHF) will be the recipient of all monies raised through the sale of this book. The Flight acts as a living memorial to all who served in the Royal Naval Air Service or Fleet Air Arm, particularly those who gave their lives in the service of their country.

The RNHF operates three Fairey *Swordfish*, one Hawker *Sea Fury* and one Hawker *Sea Hawk*, supported by a de Havilland *Chipmunk* training aircraft. The Flight is manned by 8 ex-Service civilian engineers while the aircraft are flown by serving Naval pilots, all of whom have full-time appointments elsewhere and thus give freely of their spare time. The challlenges of keeping the Flight in operaion are many and varied, but finance is a key area. The Ministry of Defence puts about half the amount needed into the kitty, while the remainder is derived from generous sponsorship by both individuals and industry, together with donations, legacies, fundraising initiatives and sales of merchandise.

www.royalnavyhistoricflight.org.uk

The *FLY NAVY* Heritage Trust

The Fly Navy Heritage Trust was formed in 1991 with the object of raising funds to ensure the continued operation of the Royal Navy Historic Flight to enable it to display its historic naval aircraft across the United Kingdom and advance the public's awareness of the Fleet Air Arm's naval aviation history and heritage. Reflecting the initial urgency to preserve the iconic Fairey *Swordfish* torpedo bomber, the Trust was set up initially as 'The Swordfish Heritage Trust' but renamed in 2002 to better encapsulate what the Fleet Air Arm is and what it does.

By striving to educate members of the public and serving personnel in the history and traditions of the Fleet Air Arm, the Trust aims to raise the FAA's profile and preserve its splendid reputation. Its history is enriched with many examples of courage and self-sacrifice - an inspiration to young and old alike. The lineage of heroic events, many further enhanced with the award of high honours, is catalogued in the Fleet Air Arm Museum, while the Memorial Church of St Bartholomew with its moving Roll of Honour completes the elements of our 'shop window' at the Royal Naval Air Station Yeovilton, the busiest military airfield in Western Europe.

Trustees are drawn from Defence Aerospace leaders and aviation enthusiasts who dedicate themselves to our twin objectives of promoting, especially in the young, an interest in naval aviation and its history as well as raising the funds to allow us to continue this work

They welcome both your interest and support, and if you are in a position to give it, your more practical assistance in terms of financial support or support in kind. You can make a difference by joining the FNHT support group, donating a minimum of £20 per annum by standing order. Visit *www.fnht.org* for more information, or write to FNHT at RNAS Yeovilton, Ilchester, Somerset, BA22 8HT.

INTRODUCTION

Rear Admiral Sir Robert Woodard KCVO   848 Sqn

The Jungly story is one of innovation, enterprise and courage. It produced a force which achieved remarkable results in some very strange places around the globe - from Malaya and Borneo in the east, Norway and the Arctic Circle to the north, the Falklands in the far south, followed by Kuwait, Iraq and Afghanistan...

The heroes who flew those S55 *Whirlwind* Mk22 helicopters in Malaya in 1952, during the Emergency, were the original 'Junglies'. This nickname stuck, because they were an intrepid band of aviators who learned to operate their helicopters over deep jungle purely by their experiences! 848 NAS (Naval Air Squadron) built up an enviable reputation for flexible efficiency with the Army, in particular the Gurkhas. A day's march in the thickest jungle was merely a few minutes flight in a helicopter. The RAF relieved 848 in 1956, having been passed on some helpful tips and lessons learned.

In 1959, the first Commando carrier, HMS *Bulwark*, was commissioned and began a long and historic line of Commando carrier operations in the Far and Middle East, which carry on to this day. The concept was the brainchild of Admiral of the Fleet Lord Louis Mountbatten. His decisions bore witness to the excellent results achieved by helicopters operating from strike carriers during the Suez crisis, as well as other events when rotary-wing aircraft from assorted units were brought together to operate in a shipborne, troop-carrying role.

848 NAS, in which I was a Sub Lieutenant pilot, re-appeared in Malaya in 1960, a month before the end of the Emergency; we were given a huge welcome by our old Gurkha friends. During the rest of that year, some large assault exercises were carried out, with *Bulwark* landing 42 Commando Royal Marines in Borneo and then a similar evolution being performed with a Gurkha unit. Three years later came the Indonesian Confrontation of 1963, and exercise theory became operational reality when the Commando and the Ghurkhas were landed in Borneo by both *Bulwark* and *Albion*. For

the next few years, the Commando Squadrons based at Nanga Gaat, deep in the jungle, earned their spurs the hard way. Their tasking was onerous - lifting patrols in and out of areas of interest, carrying out resupply and casualty evacuation, and always being ready to respond in an emergency. Their reputation was huge, especially with the Special Air Services (SAS). These historic links were further strengthened nearly twenty years later during the 1982 South Atlantic Conflict.

The release of this book has been arranged to co-incide with the 100th anniversary of the Fleet Air Arm, in May of 2009, based on the date when the order was placed for the first Naval aircraft, *HMA1*, the 'Mayfly'. The Fleet Air Arm story is in itself quite remarkable, since many of the innovations and inventions allowing ships to operate aeroplanes at sea in the worlds' naval forces emanated from the Royal Navy. Imaginative men saw both a need and a tool that could be used, then set about making the whole thing work.

The 'Jungly' force has existed for a little over half of that period; throughout that half-century, it has evolved aircraft and tactics to satisfy the needs of the Navy's soldiers, the Royal Marines. These elite troops are designed to be the first on the scene in any conflict, and without the mobility and surprise that the helicopter offers them would find their tasks much more difficult. To be placed fresh into an ideal tactical position within a fast-developing operational scenario - and then re-supplied whenever required - confers immense advantage to the local military commander.

I'm very proud to have been a 'Jungly' myself, and also very pleased to be associated with this little book, which tells a few of the stories that happened along the way...

CONTENTS

Early Junglies

Junglies at play

Junglies on Home Turf

Junglies in the South Atlantic

Cockpit is the Flight Safety magazine of the Fleet Air Arm; where 'mishaps' are concerned, it acts as an unofficial historian of the Service.

EARLY JUNGLIES

AN OVERALL VIEW

Cdr Nick Foster / Lt Cdr John Beattie CHF 1952 on

One of the key warfighting skills of the Royal Navy in the 21st century is Amphibious Warfare; a major part of that specialty involves the use of helicopters. The Fleet Air Arm was instrumental in pioneering the use of the helicopter in the early days, although the first Naval helicopter squadron formed in 1947 as an Anti-Submarine Trials unit. Their first real use in support of ground forces was put to the test during the Malayan Emergency from 1952, where *Whirlwind HAR 1* and *HAR 2* helicopters of 848 Naval Air Squadron provided support to the Army in the jungles of Malaya.

After this inauspicious start it was not long before a true amphibious capability began emerging. 845 Sqn had reformed with helicopters in 1955, and the following year embarked ten *Whirlwind HAR 3s* in HMS *Theseus* for a work-up in the Mediterranean with the Royal Marines. For the Suez operation, 845 Squadron in HMS *Theseus* was joined in Malta by 300 Royal Marines of 45 Commando. A similar light fleet carrier, HMS *Ocean*, carried 12 helicopters of the Joint Helicopter Development Unit with *Sycamores* and *Whirlwinds* plus the remainder of 45 Cdo. The initial assault plan involved landing craft, with further 'carrier borne' marines serving as an airmobile reserve.

At 0745 on 6 November 1956, the first *Whirlwind* took off from HMS *Theseus*, and then landed the CO of 45 Cdo RM near the western breakwater of Port Said. Ten minutes later the six *Sycamores* and six *Whirlwinds* from HMS *Ocean*, plus the remaining nine *Whirlwinds* from *Theseus* began launching in support. The twenty-two helicopters made history with the first British 'Vertical Assault' and completed their task in 89 minutes - 650 Commandos and 23 tons of combat supplies. This was no mean feat considering the underpowered helicopters of those days.

Although the Suez affair ended in political failure, it was a significant and pioneering military success for the Royal Navy. All combat troops had been brought in by sea, and then delivered ashore by helicopter; close air support for the ground forces had been provided by carrier-borne, naval fixed wing jet aircraft. These elements were the vanguard of a new form of amphibious warfare.

The lessons were not lost on the Government of the day, which set about establishing amphibious forces capable of rapid deployment and response. Steps towards the first Commando helicopter squadron began with the formation of 728 Sqn (Commando Flight), with four pilots and four *Whirlwinds* on 8 Jan 1958. The Flight was the logical outcome of 845 Squadron's action at Suez and 848 's experience in the jungles of Malaya some years before. It successfully conducted trials with Royal Marines in Malta and North Africa, developing troop drills, underslung load compatibility and tactical navigation to remote sites by day and night. These basic techniques and requirements remain the core of Commando Pilot training today.

728 Sqn further developed its operational procedures when it was deployed from Malta to Cyprus as 45 Heliforce (120 men of 45 Cdo and four helicopters), and was actively employed on Internal Security duties. At the same time, 845 Sqn (still in the Anti Submarine role), was embarked in HMS *Bulwark*. With a deteriorating situation in Aden, the ship was deployed there with 300 troops, and 845 again became engaged in military support operations ashore. Eventually, 728 (Commando) Flight, was expanded and re-commissioned as 848 Naval Air Squadron on 14 Oct 58. Within another two years *Bulwark* was converted to become the first LPH (Landing Platform Helicopter).

The development of this new 'Commando Carrier' concept proceeded, with its first true operational test in 1961 when the Sheikh of Kuwait asked for British military assistance to counter a growing Iraqi threat – history does repeat itself! The speed with which 600 Royal Marines and their equipment were landed ashore proved the effectiveness of this method of deploying military forces.

845 and 846 were also reformed as Commando squadrons in April and May 1962, and *Albion*'s conversion to become the second Commando carrier was completed in August. This ship, with *Whirlwind* HAS 7s of 846 Squadron and twelve of the new *Wessex* HAS 1s of 845, was soon in action transporting troops from

Singapore to Borneo to help quell both a rebellion in Brunei and the subsequent Indonesian-inspired insurrection. Over the next two years, these two squadrons worked from the ship and forward bases in the jungle in support of the army and civil population. Their performance in this challenging environment earned them lasting respect from the Army and the admiring nickname of 'Junglies', a descriptive and accurate label by which they are still proudly known today.

The arrival of the twin-engined *Wessex HU5* gave the Junglies a much increased capability; the new helicopter was soon in action with 848 Squadron in the Radfan area of Aden, and also in the continuing task in Brunei and Borneo until 1966. From 1969, the Junglies entered a rather different theatre – the Arctic. The Northern Flank of NATO was recognised as a strategically vital area during the Cold War, and the Royal Marines were a vital element in its timely reinforcement in time of tension or war. Training both aircrew and maintainers to operate effectively in the harsh environment of winter inside the Arctic Circle is a demanding task that has been under continuous development since then. All Commando Squadron personnel are rotated through a demanding AWT (Arctic Warfare Training) course in North Norway at RNoAF Bardufoss.

A detachment of four RN *Wessex 5* was also based at RAF Aldergrove for much of the Northern Ireland 'troubles'.

During the South Atlantic Conflict of 1982 (also known as 'The Falklands War'), 3 Cdo Bde Royal Marines were supported by the Commando Squadrons, which played a vital role in winning the the land battles that followed the largest amphibious landing since D-Day in World War 2. Friday May 21st 1982 saw over five tousand commandos and paratroopers, with supporting artillery and anti-aircraft missile units put safely ashore - despite intense Argentine fast jet opposition.

846 Squadron had introduced the *Sea King HC4* into service in 1979, and were embarked in various ships of the Task Force. They had just started operational flying using Night Vision Goggles (NVG), which proved very important in Special Forces operations and are now used in all night work. The *Sea King 4* also earned its spurs with casualty evacuation, transport of combat supplies, troop lifts and the key role of moving and supplying

ammunition to the artillery supporting the final assault on Port Stanley. The *Wessex 5*'s of 845, 847 and 848 Squadrons also deployed to the South Atlantic in a variety of ships, and performed to their traditional high standards, despite the loss of one whole Flight of 848 Squadron in the freighter *Atlantic Conveyor*.

In 1983/84, the Junglies of 846 and their *Sea Kings* were back in action again during the crisis in Lebanon, assisting the British forces and evacuating many civilians from Beirut.

In 1988 the *Wessex* was retired from front-line service, and many of the airframes went into deep storage. CHF - the Commando Helicopter Force - now consisted of three *Sea King 4* squadrons of eight aircraft each, with 845 and 846 designated as 'front line', and 707 in the training role.

The Gulf War of 1991 saw 845, 846 and a reformed 848 Squadron engaged in Operation *Desert Storm,* working with both 1 (UK) Armoured Division, as well as the ships at sea in the Persian Gulf. That conflict saw the rapid development and deployment of an effective electronic defensive aids suite for the CHF, which included missile approach warners, active jamming and flare decoy systems.

That war had barely finished (and indeed the squadrons were still sailing home) when duty called again, this time with 3 Commando Brigade to Operation *Haven*, where the Junglies were tasked to provide assistance to the Kurdish refugees from helicopter bases in Turkey. At the same time other aircraft were deployed to Bangladesh to facilitate disaster relief after a devastating cyclone.

The helicopter support capability to 3 Commando Brigade Royal Marines was expanded further when the *Lynx 7* and *Gazelle AH 1* of 3 Commando Brigade Air Squadron recommissioned as 847 Naval Air Squadron in 1995. 848 reformed again in 1995, this time by an identity change for 707 Squadron, but now with a wider remit than pure training, to include the specialist helicopter support of UK Maritime Counter-terrorism operations.

Throughout the 90's they have supported UK, UN and NATO ground forces in the Balkan Theatre, where 845 was the longest serving military unit between 1992 and 1998. During the early years of UN support in Bosnia, the Junglies deployed with an all-white UN paint scheme, which was soon followed by a distinctive disruptive green and white livery. Operations were conducted in Croatia, Bosnia and Kosovo throughout this period.

The Second Gulf War of early 2003 saw 845 and 846 playing a major role in the first combat night amphibious assault into the Al Faw Peninsula. Subsequent operations in Iraq have seen all three front-line Squadrons (845, 846 and 847) deployed for extended periods, again with 845 being the longest serving unit in that theatre. The dangeous nature of their duties was emphasized in 2006 when 847 tragically lost their Commanding Officer to enemy action.

In parallel, 846 bore the initial brunt of RN helicopter support to operations in Afghanistan, although 845 have also deployed now to that region. Enhanced engine modifications and a revolutionary new rotor-blade design have significantly increased the *Sea King* 4's power and performance in the hot and high altitudes of Afghanistan. However, as the Sea King 4 approaches its thirtieth birthday in Jungly service, a cost-effective successor is being looked for with some urgency. Possible contenders have included the Bell-Boeing *V22 Osprey*, the giant *CH53E*, Sikorsky *S92* and the Eurocopter *NH90*. It is more likely however, that we will see *Chinook* and *Merlin* as the replacement aircraft for this uniquely skilled amphibious helicopter force, in order to retain commonality and associated economies of training and spares with the RAF Support Helicopter units that support the Army on land.

The years since the first Jungly squadron formed have seen a concept born, developed and proved in every theatre - temperate, jungle, desert and snow. Their place in the Royal Navy is as important as ever, and this was assured by the building of the first purpose-built Commando Ship, HMS *Ocean*, followed by the replacement LPDs, HM Ships *Bulwark* and *Albion*, which together provide the cornerstone of the nation's amphibious capability.

Since 1958 the Junglies have established themselves as a major force in the Royal Navy, who have (uniquely) been actively involved in every major emergency, action or conflict since then. The helicopters have changed over the years, but the determination and the renowned 'can do' attitude of the force remains paramount, and continues to attract the admiration, respect and gratitude of all the military units that they support.

HELICOPTER GUNSHIP

Lt Tony Wilson   848 Sqn   1960

In July 1960, whilst in Singapore and thoroughly enjoying a tour with 815 Squadron in HMS *Albion*, Bill Flynn and I received 'pierhead jumps' to 848 Squadron in HMS Bulwark for what were described as 'operational reasons', as she headed off to Mombasa with her complement of *Whirlwind 7* helicopters and Royal Marines.

This was quite a shock to the system for us 'pingers', but in very short order we retrained from the anti-submarine role to that of Commando helicopter pilots. Following our arrival in Mombasa this included training in the specialist role of 'helicopter gunship', although I don't believe the term had come into general use at that time. In looking at the various ways in which the *Whirly 7* could provide aerial fire support to ground troops, the best that could be managed at the time was to bolt two fixed .303 inch machine guns beneath the aircraft. The sighting arrangements were primitive, being merely a chinagraph cross on the windscreen to give a rough idea where the aeroplane was pointing. A crew of two armourers was also carried in order to reload the machine guns as required.

With the guns fixed in position, the only way they could be brought to bear on a possible enemy ground target was with the aircraft pointing in the right direction and its nose lowered in a shallow dive. This meant climbing high enough initially to point the guns earthwards, thereby sacrificing all the advantages of keeping in cover by flying below tree top height and behind hills, as we had been taught so recently.

I should also point out that this low flying was also enormous fun and far better than sitting 'in the dip' looking for submarines and wondering where our own ship had gone! The climb up for the dive made one's aircraft a sitting duck for any return fire from the ground, and rendered the overall value of the armament somewhat debatable!

Thus it was that on 7 September 1960, using XN261, I was detailed to carry out a practise strafing sortie. The technique employed was to climb to 1000 feet, reduce speed to 35 knots, then wing over into a power-off dive, lining up on the target and firing in short bursts to adjust the aim according to the fall of shot. Every fifth round was tracer to give you an idea where the stream of bullets was was going. The dive had to be broken off no lower than 400 feet, and well before that if maximum speed was reached.

The *Whirlwind* in the dive was a very unstable gun platform, making it difficult to line up the chinagraph cross 'gunsight' with the target. Speed built up very quickly, and pulling out of the comparatively high-speed dive had to be done extremely carefully to avoid stalling the rearward-going rotor blade. As always, the great additional danger in firing weapons from aircraft at ground targets is that of 'target fixation', a phenomenon where one is concentrating so hard on the target that you forget all about the uprush of Mother Earth!

Diving towards the ground, spraying machine gun bullets generously all over the African bush, I struggled in vain to get my fire anywhere near the target, even though frustratingly I seemed to be making the right corrections.

I fired, adjusted, fired, adjusted again and so on. However, on one pass I suddenly became aware that I was already well below 400 feet and that my speed was just passing the maximum permitted. I eased back on the cyclic stick, but the seriousness of my situation unconsciously transmitted to my right hand and it moved the cyclic much too quickly, because as the nose came up, the rearward going rotor blades stalled out.

The aircraft pitched up and then rolled violently and very rapidly to the left. What happened next is none too clear. Unlikely though it might be, I'm convinced that for a moment or two the aircraft was completely upside down, and I may even have been the first to complete (and survive) a flick roll in a *Whirlwind 7*!

Rapid juggling of the cyclic and collective recovered the situation and seconds later, somehow or other, the aircraft was flying straight and level once again, though only a few feet clear of the bush - with me having very little idea of how we had managed to remain in the air. The two armourers in the main cabin had had an unnerving experience, and their stream of abusive and unseemly remarks rather succinctly and clearly expressed their opinins of my flying ability, and also introduced me to a range of expletives that thus far I had been unfamiliar with.

However, apart from my bruised pride, no damage was done to personnel or Her Majesty's property. A lesson was learned, and I kept a much more watchful eye on the altimeter and airspeed indicator in the dive thereafter. Strange though it may seem, my shooting then became less accurate than it had been previously!

A BAD CASE OF THE SHAKES

From a Cockpit Magazine article   1964

Two *Wessex 1* pilots were briefed to airlift a small Army detachment from Sibu to Song and back during the Borneo Confrontation. The task was completed without incident and both aircraft landed, taxied into the dispersal - and then ended up as total wrecks!

The first *Wessex* landed on and then ground-taxied, but space in the dispersal was very restricted indeed, and so it was common practice for a pilot to keep his rotors engaged - with the manual throttle opened to maintain 220 rotor rpm at the 'Flight Idle' setting. However, this particular aircraft could only maintain 205 Rrpm with the 15,500 compressor rpm achievable at Flight Idle. This was most unusual. So, in order to achieve 220 Rrpm, the throttle had to be opened to 17,000 Crpm, a sort of 'Flight Idle Plus'.

Meantime the second *Wessex* was also being jockeyed into dispersal. Because of the lack of space, the ploy here was for the second aircraft to turn through 180 degrees in the throat of the dispersal area, shut down and then get pushed back on to its spot. The second aircraft landed normally, but the pilot had difficulty in unlocking his tail wheel, and although he was unaware that his tail wheel was not properly unlocked and castoring, both he and the marshaller stated that the aircraft turned without difficulty - and in answer to the marshaller's signals. The Line Chief noticed that the tail wheel was not actually castoring, and subsequent examination showed that the tail wheel lock selector was 'IN' and the locking pin was actually engaged.

The rotor disc clearance during this manoeuvre was estimated variously to be between two and eight feet, very close in any language. Having passed the point which he judged to be closest to the other *Wessex*, the second pilot felt a slight judder, but did not hear or feel anything which would indicate that his blades had struck an object. Nevertheless, the judder was not normal, so he applied both brakes hard, whereupon the aircraft started to vibrate and 'pad', rocking from side to side on its undercarriage oleos. As he considered this to be incipient ground resonance, a very dangerous instability, he closed his engine HP (high pressure) fuel cock to stop the driving force to the rotor head, despite the fact that he still had 220 Rrpm set.

Ground resonance, as the name implies, is due to a resonant frequency being set up between the ground and a helicopter's rotor system, with increasing amplitude - in other words, it gets worse *very* quickly. There is normally some form of trigger to start this process, and it is true that an inherent vibration in the rotor - or perhaps 'soft' undercarriage oleo legs - are the most likely triggers. It is also more probable at certain rrpm settings than others, and it is also true to say that it is less likely at normal operating rrpm. The condition is cleared either by breaking contact with the ground, or else changing the rotor speed by 10% or more.

The second *Wessex* pilot closed his HP cock to take this latter action, influenced by a previous experience some six weeks earlier when an aircraft in which he was the co-pilot had been in a state of incipient ground resonance - and was saved by quickly shutting the HP cock and slowing the rotors down.

A witness to this accident, watching from a distance of some 200 yards, stated that at no time was the second *Wessex*'s rotor disc disturbed, and neither was he able to detect any signs of 'padding' or incipient ground resonance. When the pilot of the first *Wessex* decided that the other had reached its final position, he commenced his own shut-down procedure. While switching off his various systems, he closed the throttle to 'flight idle', and his Rrpm reduced to 205 due to the low setting of that particular aircraft's flight idle stop. At that point, his aircraft started to vibrate violently, and believing that a major defect had occurred - he closed the HP cock. Before he had time to apply the rotor brake and thus slow the rotors, the resonance increased, and his aircraft rolled to starboard, colliding with the second *Wessex* and causing heavy damage to both aircraft. The occupants abandoned both aircraft, and luckily suffered no injury as a result of their experience.

The main cause of the accident, the Board of Inquiry reported, was ground resonance - which was triggered by interaction of the downwash of the second *Wessex* that had taxied unnecessarily close, upsetting the airflow through the discs. The resonance was aggravated by the first aircraft being both light on its undercarriage and having reduced Rrpm at the unusually low flight idle setting. At one stage during the return flight the pilot had noticed some rotor vibration, but considered it to be of no significance. Upon landing, a witness (and fellow helicopter pilot) had noticed a tendency for this aircraft to oscillate on its oleos while it was taxying, and three other pilots had found the aircraft unusually 'powerful and light', and liable to skid sideways during rotor engagement.

Postscript: There was evidence of an exceptionally high engine compressor rpm (17,000) being required on on the ground in order to obtain 220 rotor rpm, which indicated too great an angle of attack on the rotor blades. As the aircraft had recently had all four blades and the main gearbox changed, it was assumed that the 'set up' was incorrect. An aircraft light on its oleos whose rotors were decelerating through a resonance 'zone' would require very little in the way of a trigger to set the resonance going. The second Wessex provided that precise stimulus.

NANGA GAAT

Sub/Lt Iain MacKenzie   **848 Sqn**   **1965**

In June 1965 I joined 848 Sqn C Flight at Nanga Gaat in Sarawak, full of beans and ready for anything. The Gaat had a wonderful reputation for seat-of-the-pants flying, as well as overcoming the many problems in life in the best traditions of Indiana Jones or Crocodile Dundee. The Army and Royal Marines raved about the service they got in all weathers and conditions, so you can imagine how excited I was about my new Squadron, its new aircraft and our future operations.

The good news was that we were flying the brand new *Wessex Mark 5* with two engines, computers to replace the considerable manual dexterity required operating a manual throttle, Auto Stabilisation Equipment (a sort of auto pilot, but not quite 'hands off' capability) and lots of other goodies. It could lift almost anything that the troops wanted lifting, had a useful load of usually 12 troops, but seating for up to 16. However, one seat was always known as the 'dead man's' seat and was never used. I can only imagine that it put the aircraft out of the acceptable Centre of Gravity range, so for the life of me I can not fathom out why it was even part of the standard aircraft fit. Of course, we would never question the integrity of a firm that also made garage doors!

Tasking hours for the *Wezzy* 5s in those early days were strictly controlled by the gilded staff somewhere far away from the front line; they made decisions based on data we could only dream about, and often limited the work our customers required of us. However, the not-so-good news at this point in my career was that stuck in a corner of the lower pads at Nanga Gaat was a very old and decrepit-looking *Whirlwind 7*, left over from the days of 846, and over which there were no limitations on flying hours provided it could be kept serviceable.

As a Midshipman, and then Acting Sub-Lieutenant, I had flown *Dragonflies* on the Search And Rescue Flight at Culdrose, and then a year flying *Whirlwind 7s* in the Far East from *Ark Royal*. As I was still a Sub-Lieutenant and most definitely in the lowest part of the food chain, guess who was 'volunteered' to fly the *Whirlwind* by my Senior Pilot whenever the occasion arose?

I did take some perverse delight in being different, in that I had two strings to my bow, and the *Whirlwind* wasn't all that bad. It was a bit like the days when you had mastered the 'crash' gearbox of the Austin Seven. Although the car wasn't wonderful, making it drive along smoothly without the grinding of gears was actually quite satisfying. Flying the *Whirlwind* over primary jungle in hot and high conditions made for some exciting times, and getting it to do some of its tasks was demanding, but also rewarding. It isn't easy to explain to a non-aviator the intricacies of helicopter aerodynamics and engine performance in a sentence or two, but trust me - the *Whirlwind* was right on the edge. This 'edge' is the difference between just being able to go flying - and crashing! It all involved a fair bit of skill and intuition, courage - and luck...

On some hot days, just to get airborne, you had to start on the lower pad at the Gaat and then reposition - empty - to the upper pad, which was on slightly higher ground and certainly well above the *Anchor Inn*, our watering hole. There you would take on fuel, embark your passengers (maximum 2, depending on fuel needed for the mission), get into a low hover, and then use the aerodynamic advantage of 'ground cushion' to creep towards the edge of the pad at full power. Then you launched yourself into a dive down the slope towards the Ragan river.

You certainly didn't have sufficient power to hover, but as you got more forward speed you actually needed less power to stay airborne, and therefore more thrust was available to help you accelerate. The critical numbers were about 15 knots to start getting an apparently amazing boost in lift, and 50 knots as the most efficient speed you could possibly achieve. At this magical figure you had the maximum amount of power available for climbing. Once clear of all obstructions and with a healthy margin of speed your problems were over - until the landing of course!

One of my more hilarious moments happened in April of 1966. We had by this stage moved to Bario in the Fifth Division, and I had now been promoted to the rather grand position of Flight Commander, 848 C Flight. Even though I was still only a Sub-Lieutenant, I had four shiny *Wessex* 5s and the old *Whirlwind 7* under my command - I have to say this would not happen in the modern Navy!

On 15 April I was tasked to fly from Jesselton to the higher slopes of Kota Belut for an Army reconnaissance mission. Given the somewhat serious weight limits for the poor old *Whirlwind* there was no space for a crewman, just the excellent maintainer Chief Petty Officer Mathieson. He was more a vital member of our crew than the aircrewman, for if the aeroplane broke down, which it often did, he would fix it!

One of the tasks on this particular day was to collect a rather tubby Major from a grid reference, and fly him on an airborne recce over territory he obviously knew fairly well from the map, but would see very little of from the back, looking sideways through the doorway at only one half of the world. He obviously had to sit up in the front cockpit alongside me.

At pick-up point, as so often happened, the terrain was sloping, there was little room among the 180 ft high trees and no place to land, so I spent some time and precious fuel looking for the best option to collect my passenger. I managed a low hover with one wheel perched on a rock, having briefed Chief Mathieson to jump out, stick a headset on the good major and tell him to climb up the left side of the aircraft and into the co-pilot's seat. While (to me at least) this seemed a very simple solution to the problem, it turned out not to be such a good plan.

The Army in those days didn't use helicopters much, and were not in the habit of getting into them, front or back. The Major, who as I may have mentioned was slightly overweight in the first place, managed eventually to start climbing towards the cockpit up the undercarriage leg and onto the purpose built steps. However, when he got to the point where his head popped into view and I was able to see his grinning face, but unable to talk to him of course, he ran out of obvious handholds! Then, using Army initiative and instinct, he found this suitably-placed horizontal lever and started to use it to haul himself up and into the aircraft.

Now the *collective* lever that he was grabbing is the flying control that causes the helicopter to go up and down - and in that sense too. Pull up the collective and the aircraft rises, lower it and the aircraft descends. The *Whirlwind* had a maximum of 44 inches of engine boost, maintained carefully and delicately with its manual throttle to provide 213 rotor rpm, which was the most efficient rotor speed. More or less rotor rpm and you got less lift, conversely, less boost and you didn't maintain the rotor rpm!

In my situation, I was pulling all of those 44 inches and the revs were exactly 213 just to maintain the hover with the one wheel on the rock - and now staring a seemingly demonic Major in the eye. There then followed a mad few minutes, which should be encapsulated in a *Roadrunner* cartoon one day, with me hauling up on the collective, trying to maintain revs and rotor pitch to keep us airborne - with the Major inadvertently and unknowingly doing his best to drop us down a rather nasty and very steep slope. Each time he heaved, the pitch would reduce, the aircraft sink onto its wheel a bit, then I would haul even harder to raise us a little, the rotor speed would go down in response, and we would sink again...

Why the Major didn't fall off is still a mystery, but eventually he made it and I was able to control the *Whirlwind* normally, albeit sitting in a pool of sweat. Dare I say, had I been in a classroom with a chalk and board I would still have struggled to explain the enormity of our situation to him, such was his understanding of matters technical!

Fortunately, it all ended well, and even more fortunately, the *Whirlwind* was taken away from us not too long after!

DOUBLE ENGINE FAILURE

2nd Lt Paul Belding RM   848 Sqn   1969

I was one of the few Royal Marine 'Specialist Helicopter Pilots', so after basic officer and Green Beret training at Lympstone I joined my Royal Navy contemporaries for flying training on the *Chipmunk, Hiller 12* and *Whirlwind 7*. I was of course, as a Marine, destined for the Jungly world, and completed Advanced and Operational training on the relatively new *Wessex 5*, which we all regarded as the 'Rolls-Royce' of helicopters.

This wonderful beast had a twin-engine installation, unlike our 'pinger' counterparts who were then flying the single engine *Wessex 1* or *3*. Like any good student, I tried hard to understand all they were telling me in ground school, but like many others, I didn't fully haul in the complexities of the computer that controlled the *Gnome* turbine engines, or the over-speed trip that was a feature of their control. The system was designed to provide balanced power from both engines to maintain the rotor head at 230 RPM. We didn't generally understand computer technology in those days; there were no such things as personal computers, not even electronic calculators, but the kit worked fairly well in service.

I should have listened a little more attentively to the lesson on 'runaways' and how to determine whether an engine had runaway 'up' or 'down', for in either case the other engine would do its level best to compensate - and still provide only the total power required.

I suppose I had around 100 hours on type by the time I joined 848 Squadron in Singapore. However, joining was via an RAF *Britannia*, and on arrival there were a few nasty surprises. The Squadron were fairly well off for pilots, and about to set off for exercises in HMS *Bulwark*. Naturally I didn't have any operational

14

experience nor was I 'theatre familiarised' having not been indoctrinated into flying in the Far East. This was a bit of a blow, in that my chum Jack Lomas and I then spent three months without flying, or more accurately, without piloting a *Wessex 5*.

We were therefore mis-employed as aircrewmen, which involved navigating and operating the back of the aeroplane, embarking and disembarking the troops, conning the pilot onto difficult landing sites, sorting out underslung loads and that sort of thing. It could not last forever of course, but was first-class experience, and eventually we got to HMS *Simbang*, that wonderful old colonial barracks and airfield at Nee Soon village on Singapore Island.

Here, my in-theatre familiarization started. This included several trips with the Squadron Qualified Helicopter Instructor (QHI) who introduced me to the differences between operating in temperate England and the hot and steamy jungle of Malaya. One sortie was my first solo Navex up into Malaya, though only solo as far as pilots were concerned, for in the left seat was Miles Cullen, an Observer, and in the back we had Bob Hitchman, my Aircrewman. I took off, full of the joys of Spring, and transited across the Straits at Johore Bahru at a sedate 90 knots and 1,000 feet, careful to maintain the correct course and not miss any of the few navigational features in what was expected to be a sea of green jungle vegetation. Air Traffic Control asked me to descend to 500 feet for a while, to deconflict with other aircraft, but a few miles further on cleared me back to 1000 ft. A few miles inland, around Ulu Tiram, there were two weapons firing ranges, and my course took me between them, but I was safe in the knowledge that they weren't noted as 'active' on this particular day, and the corridor between didn't infringe either danger area.

I started my climb back to 1000 ft and then noticed, out of the corner of my right eye, a sudden movement - then saw a Hawker *Hunter* jet fighter flash past, busily firing rockets at a target on the range. He was **very** close...

I'd been trained on the *Hiller* and *Whirlwind*, both of which had a manual throttle. As a result of flying them, one developed a very sensitive ear for the aircraft's rotor speed, and you became aware immediately this changed. Here, I was in a very unfamiliar area, and having just been scared witless by the close proximity of a fast jet, firing air-to-ground rockets, I was now hearing the most frightening noise from my rotor system, and it was a *very* definite increase.

Ground school, back at Culdrose in Cornwall, had gone into some detail about how to analyse computer problems leading to engine runaways. I looked in panic at the instrument panel, and instantly decided I had one engine run away up, because it was indicating a fuel flow of 800 lbs/hr, whilst the other engine was ticking over with a much lower fuel flow.

I tried to control the rotor RPM by raising the collective pitch lever, but it didn't seem to make much difference. I quite definitely had a runaway engine, and was very concerned at the integrity of the rotor head, so shut down the high-revving port engine using the HP cock. The rotor speed came down quite quickly and the idling starboard engine now got back into the game - and ran up to power the rotors to 230 RPM, but (sadly) I then realised that I had pulled the lever up too far - and so lowered it again, removing all the pitch (and thus drag) from the rotor blades...

The good (starboard) engine didn't know this, and simply tried its level best to give me 230 rotor RPM. The rising crescendo of noise gave me the impression that it was also out of control, so I pulled its HP cock too. I now had to make sure that I really was in autorotation, and also looked around hurriedly for somewhere to land. My options were rather limited...

Luckily, there was a small track in an oil plantation below us, and by maintaining speed at 60 knots I was able to manoeuvre the aircraft into the flare, just in time to touch down on this track - *phew*! Because of no wind, our ground roll was quite fast, and during that deceleration process the port main undercarriage hit a tree stump and was damaged, though the aircraft remained upright. On the way down, my quick thinking Observer had transmitted a *Mayday* call, which was heard by a twin-rotor RAF *Belvedere* (which we Junglies knew as the '*Flying Longhouse*'!).

We stood around our *Wessex* for a little while, listening to the hot metal-inspired tinkling noises, and chatting to a couple of small boys who miraculously appeared out of the vegetation - which they do in that part of the world at even the faintest sound of a helicopter. One of us also operated the thoughtfully provided

SARBE rescue beacon apparatus, and I still have the silver tankard to prove it!

Not too long later, the *Belvedere* thumped into view and then flew around, looking for somewhere to land - but there was no space or clearing large enough. Undaunted, and seriously intent on a rescue, quite probably with visions of medals and/or a promotion, the pilot then came into a fairly high hover and lowered a thick manila rope, with his crewman indicating that I should climb up it.

I started the climb, but only got about six feet up before working out that this was probably a good way to die. I descended again, and the crewman pulled the rope back into the cabin, to send it flying out ten minutes later, this time with knots tied every 5 ft or so. I smiled and waved up at him, then went to join my crew sitting under a nearby tree. He eventually got the message, went away and all was serenely quiet again.

Half an hour later, a Royal Navy *Whirlwind* hove into view, which could land in the clearing. I feared the worst later on when walking into the Squadron office block, but my CO patted me on the head and said it wasn't my fault; the aircraft was recovered and flew again some time later after they had repaired the damage.

The Accident Investigation Unit discovered that the port engine computer had an intermittent defect which told the throttle to go to full flow, thus initiating my problem. Unfortunately, there didn't seem to be much wrong with the starboard engine at all, and they also told me that a rotorhead speed of 285 RPM would not have caused it to fall apart.

They don't tell you that back in Ground School!

PILOT SELECTION

S/Lt John Beattie   **705 Sqn**   **1970**

We had joined the Royal Naval College at Dartmouth, fresh faced and eager to get flying, only to find that 'flying', very frustratingly, came a bit later. We did sums, sailed boats, ran up long flights of stone steps, marched around a parade ground, learned Naval History and aerodynamics, stared longingly at the only female professor (who was actually quite 'old', certainly well into her thirties), told each other how much fun it was going to be when we finally got to a Squadron, and so on. But some failed, or realised perhaps the discipline and lack of freedom wasn't for them.

Part of the 'Specialist Helicopter Pilot' curriculum was to fly the *Chipmunk* at Plymouth's Roborough airport, to be assessed as competent or not to carry on further in the Pilot Training pipeline. One of our number headed for the control tower after every take off - not a good trait in a naval aviator, so he re-streamed as an Observer. Other prospective pilots became Air Traffic Controllers or returned to the Seaman specialty because of their lack of ability. I was an ex 'lower decker' so had to go through these filters before joining BRNC Dartmouth, and as it was a leave period, I was the only student at Roborough airport at the time.

Amongst things I learned about was air sickness, fairly early on, especially when spinning; worse, no-one told me to learn the checklists by heart, so I didn't. My final handling test was put off a couple of times because of strong and very gusty winds, but eventually the grading officer decided he would assess me anyway - and make allowances for the conditions. My upper air work was uninspiring but adequate, though after a couple of huge 'Bomber Command' circuits he realised I was reading the checks from the thoughtfully-provided printed check list, therefore taking ages on the downwind leg - and ending up in a totally wrong position for the final approach to land.

He did the checks for the next couple of circuits to land, and I must have impressed him a bit because I passed with a 'C', which was the lowest possible pass. He also said I was more mature than normal students and therefore would probably manage to flannel my way through somehow!

The remnants of our course eventually passed out, and we then joined with another decimated course, plus five General List officers who had spent the previous four years on seamanship training, and became an 18-strong group at Linton-on-Ouse. Again, we were flying the *Chipmunk,* and the course was designed to teach us the basics of the various aspects of flying. In the process, they could weed out those who couldn't absorb the instruction in a reasonable time. You certainly had to apply yourself, but we also managed to major in 'social studies', as I recall.

The whole Naval section then moved from Linton to

Church Fenton, halfway through the course, an event marked by a riotous dinner at Linton. The Royal Navy had been there since 1925, so we felt it our duty to mark the occasion. An alcohol-fuelled brain can be very inventive.

We conspired to have a sign made saying '**Royal Navy gone this way**', and at around midnight, started digging in the Station Commander's prized rose bed, in front of the Mess. The hole had to be big enough for our sign, and about 5 ft deep. The Light Blue forces (RAF) would easily pull the sign out again, but as the Mess was being worked upon by builders at the time, we soon found a concrete mixer plus the correct ingredients to make ourselves a 'mix'. Twelve inebriated Naval Officers, still dressed in almost brand new and very smart formal kit, wheeling barrows full of very wet cement from the back of the mess through the foyer to the rose garden in the front, can do a lot of damage to themselves, their uniforms - and their surroundings!

Other high jinks that night included nailing up the church bell rope in the bell tower, so that on Sunday all the normal actions produced no result (it did seem funny at the time); building a 10 foot high brick wall right across the main road into the camp, just around the corner from the Guardroom; pinching every single bicycle and hiding them all on top of an accommodation block (there are very *very* many bicycles on an RAF station), and putting a brand new Volkswagen Beetle from the front-of-mess senior officers' car park up on four beer barrels, one under each wheel.

This, by pure chance, happened to belong to the RAF Group Captain in charge of Police and Security! The '*piece de resistance*' was to mark out a huge '**FLY NAVY**' in weed killer on the triangle of grass in the centre of the airfield. Two days later you could see it from 25 miles away at 6,000ft! The term '*Fly Navy*' had only been coined the previous year for the Transatlantic record attempt by Royal Navy F-4K *Phantoms* (with Lt Cdr Brian Davies winning hands down I seem to remember).

During the latter stages of the course, now at Church Fenton, I was on a navigation exercise one night and, at 1900 feet, was head down in the cockpit setting up the compass prior to rejoining the circuit. I finished this task, and looked up to see a pair of navigation lights directly in front of me and quite close, so said urgently to my instructor: "*Go down!*". His only response was to look gingerly over my shoulder - so I pushed the stick fully forward, and the nose dumped downwards, big time. He then looked up and saw the propeller of another *Chipmunk* miss our tail by about 10 feet. It seems it was another Chippy going out on a night navigation exercise, the first action of which was to do the same as I had been doing, namely the student setting up the compass! They just didn't see us at all...

Needless to say, several of our number fell by the wayside during the course, and eventually twelve of us moved on to further training, now on *Hiller* and *Whirlwind* helicopters at RNAS Culdrose. We were joined there by a couple of old salts who were re-streaming from fixed wing flying to helicopters, and a couple of 'back-coursed' students as well, and so became 18 strong again. The camaraderie amongst we students was excellent, and we conspired to help those finding things difficult, particularly by taking them away from their worries and giving them a night's relaxation in one of the local hostelries. I think it must have worked for some, but may have been the straw that broke the camel's back for others!

One of our number was practising sloping ground landings in a *Hiller* when a member of the 'senior' course taxied past in a much bigger *Whirlwind*. The stories vary, but our boy in the *Hiller* experienced what he thought was a tail rotor failure, with the aircraft swinging abruptly one way, and so took the appropriate corrective action in normal circumstances (over *flat* ground), namely lowering the collective lever and closing the throttle. The helicopter in this configuration is no longer a helicopter, but a brick, and it descended rapidly from a ten foot hover to the sloping ground, where one skid hit hard, the fuselage rolled around this now immobile structure, and the whole shebang turned over, with bits flying everywhere.

The *Hiller* student was now upside down, hanging in his straps with acid from the battery passing quite close to his head on its way to the roof of the inverted helicopter. Sizzling sounds accompanied the rhythmic beat of the *Whirlwind* taking off and going about his business, blissfully unaware of the carnage in his wake! Equally unaware was the control tower, who were certainly not in control of anything that day - despite being in direct line of vision with the top of the sloping ground area. Luckily, one of the civilian mechanics from the squadron had seen the *Hiller* and raised the alarm. I would have been delighted to report further that the fire engine turned up and covered everything (including the hapless student pilot) in foam, but alas that wasn't the case. He was simply helped out of the wreck!

To be scrupulously fair, and possibly ruin a very good story, the *Whirlwind* pilot says to this day that he came nowhere near the *Hiller*, but it was a bit of a 'twitchy' day and the *Hiller* student totally misidentified the problem. The *Hiller* pilot did go on to get his wings, but didn't do very well on the Anti-Submarine Warfare course - and eventually became a policeman.

We are very slowly drawing towards the point of the story, you'll be delighted to learn. Our course, now down to a hard core of 12 again, all desperately wanted to be Jungly pilots and join the Commando world. 'Junglies' had dash, charisma and verve, were flying the new twin engine *Wessex 5* helicopter, and we couldn't imagine anything worse than sitting in the hover at night, being told what to do by an Observer while hunting submarines in a single engined *Wessex 1* or *3*.

At the end of 705 Squadron, we were presented with our Pilot's wings, and then had to undergo a selection process for the final stage of training - and the flying specialisation that would determine the rest of our careers.

For my course there were only two choices, Anti-Submarine or Commando (there was occasionally a choice to go *Wasp*, on Frigate flights). Each of the training squadron Commanding Officers gave us a brief on what their specialisation involved, but 40 years later I still remember both as being lacklustre at best and rather uninspired. The selection process was corrupt in many ways, and involved how many were needed for each discipline, as well as whether you needed the support of another pilot or crewman, i.e. whether you were a bit immature (ASW), or whether the opposite applied and you could cope on your own (Cdo). It also mattered hugely whether the selectors, our 705 Sqn instructors, liked or hated you - and so on! Part of the process was our own personal choice. We were 12 strong - and there were six places in each camp.

Decision day drew closer. There was much discussion between us, as well as sly attempts to encourage our mates to go the other way - thus leaving a clear field for our own choice, but we *all* remained ardent 'Jungly' supporters, right up until the day before we had to cast our preferences.

During a quiet night in the bar, the six Midshipmen on our course happened to be chatting to Colin Bates, one of our instructors who was on duty. He was a lovely chap, an excellent pilot and instructor, respected by us all, and affectionately and universally known as 'Master' for obvious reasons. Sadly, he was killed in a civilian helicopter crash many years later when the machinery failed - due to a manufacturing or maintenance error.

On this particular evening, 'Master' Bates was expounding on the virtues of the brand spanking new *Sea King* HAS Mk 1, for which the Intensive Flying Trials Unit was about to form. He told of leaving the deck of a carrier or cruiser on a coal-black night in the rain, flying low over the water on instruments 100 miles from the fleet, 'dipping' the sonar body, finding and chasing a fast nuclear submarine, getting authority to attack it, dropping a homing torpedo, achieving the kill and then returning to the deck four hours later without seeing a single thing outside the window. Much was made of the capability of the *Sea King*, its range, speed, the teamwork of a crew working in harmony, the technical aspects of its autopilot which would allow it to fly 'hands off' down to the hover at any set height, maintain position over the sonar cable and then transition back to forward flight.

It was the stuff of magic. He told the tale incredibly well, and took them all along with him. They could be the *Sea King* experts of the future, because no-one knew anything about it at that time. The Fleet Air Arm had literally just received the first one minutes before! They could easily be the consummate professionals making this whole new level of operational capability work effectively...

They bought the package totally, swallowing the concept hook line and sinker. On the following day, the middies volunteered for ASW duties, all six of them! The rest of us, all Sub Lieutenants and Lieutenants, became the 6 Jungly candidates. Without some accidental help from the wonderful Colin Bates, you wouldn't be reading this book - and I may have had to slash my wrists years ago!

Just to sharpen the inter-tribal rivalry that keeps us all on our professional toes, it also has to be said that the only submarine that the RN has ever sunk in anger since then, was Argentinian, depth-charged by a *Wessex 3* and then hit with a navalised anti-tank missile from a *Wasp* in the action off South Georgia in 1982!

DOUBLE ENGINE FAILURE #2

Lt David Baston   **707 Sqn**   **1970**

This is a tale from days of old, when knights were bold and engine failures in the *Wessex 5* were more common than perhaps we would have liked. Here was this lovely new helicopter crafted out of native materials and, although based on an old American design, was very different indeed in the engine compartment. It had a twin Rolls-Royce *Gnome* installation, joined together by a coupling gearbox to power the rotor system. This gearbox had the facility to allow you to start the port engine and run generators, hydraulic and oil pumps etc. without putting any torque on the rotor system, and was a bit like an Auxilliary Power Unit (APU).

Next, you started the starboard engine, with which you could engage the rotors, then select 'Idle' on the port engine, make a switch to engage the main drive, before running the port turbine up to normal power again, but now coupled into the rotor system. Ingenious, and the 'automatics' took care of sharing the power output so that each engine provided half of that needed. In the event of one failing, the other compensated and ran up to the torque required. One engine couldn't quite give you the full effort of two, but very nearly.

One particular episode springs to mind, and taught me never to trust an Air Engineer officer ever again. John 'Puds' Shears was the 'grubber' in question, just to protect the anonymity of the rest of you! (**Puds** was his nickname for a very good reason, best left to your imagination). We were required to carry out engine 'stall margin' checks, whilst tied down to the ground, to try and sort out the failings of the inlet guide vane (IGV) actuators. Occasionally aircraft would start but when you pulled power the engine would 'stall' – and stop. The guide vanes should move under the control of an actuator as power is increased, in order to direct incoming air on the first row of the compressor blades *at the correct angle*. However, they sometimes failed miserably in their mission, and for no apparent reason.

In the halcyon days of 707 Sqn under Barry Hartwell, there was an aircraft that just would *not* pass all the ground checks, and kept having problems in the IGV area. The Air Engineering Officer (AEO) was Puds, who decided one day that they had done everything in their power, the problem was now fixed, and a full blown test flight was needed either to prove this judgement correct, or find the source of any continuing trouble. This pre-supposed that we could get both engines started OK and the rotors engaged - with no stalling, of course!

After his short search for a gullible pilot, I volunteered on the express condition that Puds flew with me in the left hand seat, to show his confidence that the maintainers had indeed fixed it this time, and as a mark of confidence in his own judgement. The test flight involved climbing on one engine at full power for so many seconds, with the other engine back at ground idle, then dumping the collective pitch lever into autorotation (zero pitch) to see what happened. Then, on passing 1000 ft on the way back down, we would pull the collective pitch lever right up, thus demanding full power again within a very few seconds.

Well on this occasion, with a very loquacious and confident Puds watching wide eyed as we careered upwards on our moon shot, followed by a brief period of weightlessness as I entered autorotation (something he hadn't felt in many a year…weightless!), the engine made a spectacular *wuffle wuffle bang* noise and stopped dead, to the accompaniment of clouds of unburnt paraffin smoke issuing from its *very* large exhaust pipe.

At this point we were over Hayle and much lower than 1000 ft, as the pressure altitude was quite different from the real world at that day's temperature. No problem thinks I, just stay in auto and advance the other engine to Flight Idle in order to take over the task of staying airborne. Then, we'll just gently raise the lever and fly away…

We were now at about 500 feet above the ground, and with the collective lever coming up smoothly and slowly - guess what? *Wuffle wuffle bang*, the spare engine also stops and the rotor revs decay like Puds's confidence. I am suddenly committed to an engine-out landing in the field below. This was not very easy, despite copious practice in those days. The helicopter **has** to come down quite quickly, in order to generate the air flow that keeps the rotors turning, whilst moving ahead at around 60 knots and trying to avoid all obstacles in its path.

At this speed you also have to manoeuvre into wind and position the aircraft onto the correct end of a flat field; in Cornwall all fields are quite definitely small. At about 100 feet above the ground, the aircraft is flared to diminish both forward speed and rate of descent, which - if accomplished at exactly the right time - should result in a run-on, after which the aircrew move to the nearest pub. There was a small problem this time with power lines in our way, but they were high enough to get the aircraft underneath at the end of the flare!

Well, we did get down all in one piece and even had just enough time to tell somebody over the radio as we neared the ground, such was my spare mental capacity in those heady days when I was young. Lovely lady comes out from a farm with tea and biscuits, the duty SAR helicopter arrives and Puds then says, *"If you can get it started, would you fly it back to Culdrose?"*

Gosh, I must have been so *so* green at that age, because I said *"Yes, as long as you come with me..."* Remember a few lines back?

Anyway, both engines start perfectly normally, rotors engage without problem, we lift into the hover and then it's **'Wuffle Wuffle Bang'** again. At this stage it seemed a good idea to land using the one engine that was still running, and then let a big lorry take our helicopter back to Puds's boys, to have another long think about it all. He agreed that he'd had enough excitement for one day, and I think that he'd also developed a little more respect for the Pilot fraternity!

MALAYAN NIGHT ASSAULT

Anonymous   848 Sqn   1971

We were in the Far East in a Commando carrier, in the days of the *Wessex 5*; despite the fact that the Squadron boasted 22 such helicopters, rarely could we fly more than about 16 because of both unserviceability and maintenance requirements. I can recall though that we were very good at daytime assaults, and on a regular basis could put our Commando of about 750 troops and supporting vehicles ashore in half the time that it took our American counterparts in similar ships, even though they were using a potentially more capable helicopter, the CH46 *Sea Knight*. We often flew at night as well, but rarely did anything other than operations with single aircraft, or close formations of up to four machines.

All this occurred well before the days of night vision goggles; we only had the naked eye. However, some bright spark, while we were on exercise off the eastern coast of Malaysia, decided that we would launch a 16 aircraft 'Notional night assault' to a jungle landing site. 'Notional' because we wouldn't carry any troops, 'night' because we didn't do it in darkness too often - and it would be very good for us - whilst the reason for the word 'assault' escapes me, as there was no enemy to oppose us!

Just getting 16 helicopters available for this evolution was quite a challenge for our engineers, but they rose to it admirably. The exercise had been planned by the staff of Flag Officer Carriers and Amphibious Ships (FOCAS), and to show their support and commitment, they now turned up to brief us.

We were to fly tactically, which in this instance meant taping off the lower part of the aircraft navigation lights so they couldn't be seen from the ground - and not using the fuselage-mounted anti-collision beacon. Thankfully, there was no ban on the use of the radios. We were to be launched ashore at one minute intervals and have an illuminated approach 'Tee' to guide us into the right place, and thence to one of four Landing Site (LS) 'spots' to touch down.

Our Royal Marines demanded that as many of them be put on the ground at the same time as was humanly possible and the rest right behind. They always expected to be poorly placed as an assault force in terms of ratio of enemy to own troops, so this strategy was constantly drummed into to us. None of us had been to this landing site before, though I guess the Squadron CO or Senior Pilot must have recce'd it prior to the exercise. Our own Mobile Air Operations Team (MAOT) would set up the LS in such a way that we could land and take-off reasonably independent of other aircraft doing the same.

The brief, by both FOCAS staff and our own Senior Pilot, was very comprehensive and much was made of the fact that we would be separated by one minute between aircraft. It was imperative that we keep this spacing, so we had to climb out at exactly 70 knots to 1000 feet and then cruise the 40 miles ashore at exactly 90 knots, descending from an Initial Point at exactly 70 knots until 500 feet above the site on the final approach. Each LS was given a colour, and we were to call 'final' on the radio for the colour we thought was empty, which was fine for the first few aircraft, but got a bit tricky later on. The MAOT boys, however, would put us right if the LS we called for was occupied.

Needless to say, it was also important to occupy a LS only for one minute, to maintain the correct spacing. Also during the brief, I was told to carry a senior member of the FOCAS staff in my left hand seat, 'just for the ride and to see how it all went'. The ship's flight deck only had nine spots to operate from at night, but we could shuffle aircraft round a bit and get eleven ranged on deck, moving the extra two once the first of the nine had gone, and then getting the other four up from the garage, blades spread and onto a spot as space became available. This was a good part of the exercise of course, integrating the Squadron engineers and flight deck party to do things in the right order and double quick time. This we excelled at.

I was No 10 or 11, and attempted to brief my passenger, who talked more than I did during my brief to him. He was an old Jungly, now too senior to hold a flying appointment, but eager to get to grips with the *Wessex* again. Alarm bells rang, and I mentally told myself that I was the Captain of the aircraft and my word was law, even though he was of an advanced age and rank and looked fairly fierce! He was late getting out to the aeroplane, causing me some agitation, though to be fair he didn't eventually hold me up in my need to get the blades spread, port engine started whilst being moved to a flying spot, and starboard engine and rotors running as soon as we were on the spot!

We lifted from the deck on time - big sigh of relief - and climbed out at exactly 70 knots, levelling and increasing to exactly 90 knots at 1000 feet as briefed. My passenger had been quiet thus far, but now got a bit talkative, advising me that he probably had more hours on the *Wessex* than I'd had hot dinners etc. I asked if he'd like to fly, and naturally he grabbed the controls immediately, and despite being beautifully in trim, caused the speed to fall to 70 knots! I said nothing for a little while, assuming he'd settle down and improve very soon. After all it was *his* FOCAS brief which had emphasized that accuracy was essential!

He didn't improve. I asked him to get the speed back to 90, whereupon he guffawed a bit and our velocity shot up to 110, but again I left it a while, mentally arguing that we'd been at 70 for a time so this 'adjustment' would make up for that. Things didn't get much better, and I was asking him to adjust speed with monotonous regularity, after a while losing the plot of how long we'd been too slow against how long too fast! Needless to say, the other aircraft probably wouldn't be visible until quite close, as it was one of those **very** dark nights, and the half-taped navigation lights wouldn't show until we were very close. I had the cockpit lighting turned down really low and was spending every spare moment staring out into the inky blackness, looking for the aircraft ahead, and attempting to navigate to the turn point on the coast and then the Initial Point (IP) for the landing site. Both of these features were rather crucial to the overall plan.

I did wrest control from my passenger in time for the descent to the landing site, unsure of where I was in relation to any other aircraft, but listening carefully to the radio to get an idea of the LS plot. An aircraft ahead called 'finals', and I adjusted speed to call the same about a minute later, but to achieve this had to fly down the glide slope at 30 knots. The get out clause for all of us was to yell "*Anti-colls!*" on the radio if we felt it necessary (scared!), whereupon everyone put on their anti-collision lights and we could see where our neighbours were. No one wanted to be the wimp who had to weaken first of course, and we all hung on as long as possible. I was on late finals to the Tee when I called for the Blue LS, to be told it was full, go for the Red.

A split second after that, the radio practically shrieked: "*Anti-colls, anti-colls*", a transmssion from someone as equally confused as me. By my reckoning, I should have only been able to see a few aircraft, but I swear I could see all sixteen! The sky all around us was full of bright red, flashing anti-collision beacons, reminiscent of the turning on of the Blackpool Illuminations! There were four aircraft on the LS, though one lifted just as I got to the Tee.

It has to be said that at night, judging the distance away of these lights was nigh on impossible. It was obvious that some had missed the site and were going round for a second try; some got there early, some stayed on the ground for more than their minute, some were on climb-out, and so on. The 'fixes' to get us all back on the straight and narrow were many and various and thank goodness for the radio, but somehow we sorted the pot mess out, landed, took off again - and soberly trudged the 40 miles back to the ship. In my case, this was at 1475 feet on the basis that nobody else would be at that ridiculous height!

My passenger seemed pleased with the whole thing, but I never fathomed out why. He was definitely an alien from a different planet. We didn't ever do it again during my time on the squadron, which I think was very sound judgement on someone's part. We did night fly again of course, because that is an essential part of the job, a truth that was never more apparent than eleven years later in the Falklands campaign, where some extremely skilled and dangerous night missions were successfully conducted with the advantages that total darkness brings.

LOADLIFTING

S/Lt Keith Copus   848 Sqn   1971 – 1972

On exercise with the bootnecks in Sardinia, we were carrying out an assault on some mythical enemy. The *Wessex 5* ahead of me was carrying a Land Rover, underslung. It was hot, and with very little wind the *Wessex* would have been pulling maximum power in the hover. This is a situation where we were able to use our skill, and indeed took great pride in doing so. The trick was to gradually reduce both height and speed in a gentle flare, to reach the landing point with none of either, all the time allowing for the load hanging underneath. Decelerating in this way used less power than trying to come to the hover. If you ended up a little short or high, you had insufficient power left. Then the whole assembly descended, and you could hurt the Landrover...

The chap in front of me on this particular day got it just right and as the Landrover wheels kissed the ground, he moved left slightly, released the hook with a switch on his cyclic stick, dropping the heavy ring on the lift strop clear of the bodywork - (and more importantly the windscreen).

Perfect, my turn next with a stick of troops, much lighter than the Landrover. I had no problems but unfortunately, as I watched during my approach, the hand-brake on the Landrover had been left off and the vehicle started to roll forward, at first very slowly and then, as the ground wasn't quite level, continued to accelerate until it ran off the edge of the ridge.

As can be imaged, Landrovers are not particularly aerodynamic, especially in a free fall of about 400 metres. Later, when the wreckage was returned to HMS *Bulwark,* the remains were about two feet high. It did have to be taken back of course, because someone had signed for it and it would have to be returned to Stores in order to get it off their charge!

A little later, on exercise off Corsica, we were putting the Commandos ashore as usual, and as it was early into the sortie we were carrying a fair amount of fuel. My *Wessex* 5 was at its Maximum All Up Weight, with a reasonable 2900 lbs of available payload. My next load from the ship was a Landrover FFR, (Fitted for Radio). This type of vehicle was the heaviest of the series, weighing around 3250 lbs. The chaps preparing it had of course filled it with all sorts of extras so they didn't have to muck about finding the stores once on the ground...

Being young and keen, I tried to lift the load - but ended up pulling maximum torque and still not going anywhere. In order to reduce the load weight, I asked the crewman to indicate to the boys beneath him who were attaching the load, to lighten it. He did all the gesticulating required and they took off the spare wheel, water jerrycans, spare fuel cans, windscreens and canopy frame. However, being Royal Marines, they then smartly threw these items into the back of the vehicle.

After all, their mates ashore would be needing them!

Later on - I can't remember the exact location - I was once again following my colleagues in an aircraft stream, most of us with underslung loads. The aircraft ahead was carrying a *Wombat* anti tank weapon. This 105 mm calibre device looked like a drainpipe, about 3 metres long, attached to a pair of wheels. It started to oscillate and swing underneath the *Wessex,* something which occasionally happened to such a light load. We could use various flying techniques to control this, such as turning, climbing, descending, or changing speed, and I could see the pilot trying all of these. Unable to get the load back under control, he eventually had to jettison it before things got really exciting and the load came up into contact with the rotor blades.

The *Wombat* departed from the lifting strop in a quite beautiful arc, maintaining a fairly level attitude initially, with no tumbling at all - and then gradually entered a curved path with all the grace and beauty of a high diver, which of course it was, whilst heading for *terra firma.* The image of that perfect curve will live in my mind forever and I cannot really find the words to describe it properly. At the end of its short first solo flight it hit the ground, with the barrel burying itself into the surface like a home-sick tent peg. There was to be no more tank-busting for that particular piece of kit!

PRESSONITIS #1

Lt John Beattie   **846 Sqn**   **1972**

It was 1972, the early days of winter deployments to the Arctic and four pilots, supported by two aircrewmen and a trio of maintainers had been tasked to take two *Wessex* from Yeovilton to Arbroath, to carry out Troop Drills with 45 Cdo in readiness for their Norway deployment the following January. We completed our tasking and then had a very 'sociable' last night's formal Christmas dinner with the RM officers who lived in the Mess, afterwards playing the stupid alcoholic games that you play when you are young and stupid!

In the cold light of morning, with throbbing heads, we discovered that the weather forecast was not wonderful, but our Yorkshire refuel stop at Leeming looked 'workable'. Yeovilton in Somerset was not yet open for business, but we were all scheduled to go on Christmas leave on arrival, so the homing instinct was very strong.

Sadly one of the very serious problems with helicopters generally and the *Wessex* in particular, is they don't like cold, wet air. The moisture freezes on the rotor blades, forming ice; this changes the shape of the airfoil section into something more akin to a plank, and can ultimately cause the helicopter to fall out of the sky. The critical numbers are about +2° C down to -15° C, which is the worst regime, and one we should definitely avoid in cloud. From memory the temperature at Arbroath was around + 2° C at ground level as we set off towards Leeming, our fuel stop, with a lowering cloudbase the further south we got. Our Senior Pilot was in the lead, a man of experience whom we respected and trusted, so all was well. We just had to follow him...

A little way down the route, it became obvious that the sky was likely to meet the ground fairly shortly, but the Met man had said the cloud tops would only be at 4000 ft, and there should be a few holes, so we elected to climb up on top. The two *Wessex* stuck close as we ascended through what started as a hole, but had closed to thin stratus by the time we got to the actual tops at 5000 ft in bright sunshine, with an outside air temperature of -7° C!

Plan good so far as we enjoyed the view of unbroken cloud beneath and blue sky above. There were only 90 miles to go, with an hour and a half's kerosene left in the fuel tanks. Someone called Yeovilton on the HF radio to get a weather update from them, but it didn't sound too hopeful, 'Amber' conditions with a slim chance of improvement, would probably mean having to do a radar approach through cloud. This was definitely not a good idea. As Leeming got closer, we started to concentrate on the problem of getting down through the cold and still unbroken cloud. Once in radio contact, Leeming gave us their weather, which was just about OK, with a cloudbase of 300 ft and 2 miles visibility.

We flew on past Leeming for some miles above the cloud when suddenly a hole appeared beneath us, and we both entered autorotation quite close together - spiralling down to the big road beneath. Someone was smiling on us, as it was the A1, which we followed back up to Leeming at around 150 ft, just below the cloud. Big sighs of relief all round as we filled the fuel tanks to the brim , and made for the Met office. I can't remember the exact details of the discussion, but it was quite obvious that the only way we were going south was if we did it on the west coast, where the air was much warmer, rather than our intended, direct track.

New plan made, we got airborne again and climbed up nervously through the cloud - to pop out on top unscathed and happy in the sunshine, now heading towards Blackpool. More HF radio traffic with Yeovilton, who had now gone 'Red', meaning we were unlikely to get in even if we got close.

OK, let's stop at Blackpool for fuel, and call the Met office at Yeovilton by telephone before launching again. We raised Blackpool Airport on the VHF radio, which only one aircraft was fitted with. They say they are in poor weather, 150 yds visibility in fog, with full cloud cover and no discernable cloudbase. They can, however, give us VHF radio bearings to get to them. Using these VDF bearings we could work out when we were over the coast and then give it a couple more minutes of westerly track to be sure.

Quick chat between aircraft on the UHF radio. First *Wezzy* will descend over the sea, using the radar altimeter to avoid hitting it, then home into Blackpool using its VHF radio. Second *Wessex* follows 10 mins later and homes in on transmissions from our UHF radio. We let down quite quickly at first to get out of the colder cloud high up, but slow our descent rate right down when going through about 700 feet. We saw the sea at about 75 feet, but with fairly poor visibility forward. Blackpool gave us bearings and we homed in towards the field, seeing the famous tower at about half a mile range, slightly on our left side...

The airfield was along the beach, so we followed the coast a little way, moving gingerly at about 60 knots and only sighting the airfield at a couple of hundred yards range. We sat on the end of the runway and transmitted on our UHF radio so that the other aircraft could home in on us using his 'Violet Picture' device. He made it, but only just, as 20 minutes later the weather worsened still more to 25 yds visibility, when neither of us would have got in. It also seems that the rest of the country had quickly and unforecastedly 'socked in' and was likely to stay that way, so alternative airfields would have been no use to us either. The fact that Blackpool was at sea level had saved our bacon.

Both aircraft were fuelled up as phone calls were made, but Yeovilton was out of limits, big time. Bournemouth was still just about OK for commercial traffic using the Instrument Landing

System, and in fact a *Herald* parked nearby was about to position there, empty... Quick negotiations got the two *Wessex* a hangar until after Christmas, and the *Herald* crew, our final ray of hope, busily negotiated with their operations staff. Sadly the insurance situation wouldn't allow passengers on a positioning flight, so two hire cars were rented, all nine of us piled in, and off we shot down the motorway.

My hire car then proceeded to boil over - and had to be swapped! We had had a very long day, with some stressful flying followed by a long drive, and pulled in through the gates of Yeovilton at 0100 in the morning, but at least we were in the right place and able to go off on Christmas leave. The Squadron CO and I then travelled up to Blackpool just before the New Year to collect the two *Wessex*, and flew back to Yeovilton under a fabulously clear blue sky in bright sunshine.

ROCKETS AWAY

Anonymous **848 Sqn** **1972**

I was nearing the end of my first tour as a Jungly pilot in 848 Squadron, embarked in HMS *Albion*. We were in the Med for a multi-national exercise in Greece, but prior to that were carrying out some training in Cyprus. On 24 April 1972 the weather was good, spirits were high and we were ready to take on the world. Our excellent Senior Pilot, Lt Cdr Peter Woodhead, who later became an Admiral, planned and briefed a programme of sorties on the range at Larnaca, using 2 inch rockets. This was always good sport, and an evolution which we thoroughly enjoyed.

I was lucky enough to be selected for the first wave of four *Wessex* 5's, with our CO, Lt Cdr Barry Hartwell, in the lead. We all carried spare pilots who would be dropped at the range control hut, whilst we departed to loose off 14 of the 28 rockets we carried. Then we were to change pilots, release the other 14 projectiles, and get back to the war canoe in order to re-arm and crew change.

A normal start was made, flying dummy attacks to get our eye in, and then we started firing. About half way through there was an urgent *"Check, check, check!"* over the radio, followed by instructions to return to the ship and de-arm. It seems that although we had all read the Range Orders and signed as having done so, there was a sentence buried in amongst the stuff about toss bombing by *Buccaneers*, that **no live RP shall be used on this range**! One of our number, recently of the fixed-wing fraternity, had read this bit out of interest.

The Range Safety Officer, a crusty old C**bfat, hadn't realised that the lovely bright orange flashes as the rockets hit were the explosive heads exploding! Good job that it was noticed, for that very afternoon, after shutting down from a very satisfying 3 hour support sortie, I was approached by the Senior Pilot again, this time on a very noisy flight deck with several aircraft running, and told to '*get in that aircraft with S/Lt Bloggs and look after him*'. Not the most extensive of briefs, but what the hell...

I rushed into the Line office, signed for my aeroplane and then ran out to it, already 'burning and turning' at the fore end of the flight deck. On approaching, I noticed that it was armed with 28 rockets, something we would normally brief separately! Never mind, I'd been in on the morning brief etc. Ducking under the rockets (we always regarded them as being *very* unsafe), I clambered up into the left-hand seat, and strapped in whilst S/Lt Bloggs grinned sheepishly. He had joined the Squadron only two weeks previously, straight from training, and seemed to be a very good chap. We took off and went to the range, this time armed with rockets that had inert heads, just a chunk of metal of the correct size, weight and shape in place of the explosive.

We started flying dummy circuits and it was all too evident that Bloggs was not flying them at all well - and was very aware of his inadequacy. It was essential that you were at the right height and speed before you tipped into a 20 degree dive, which you always did over the same ground position, each circuit you made. That way you could adjust your point of aim to account for the error you experienced on the previous shot...

After he screwed up several attempts, I suggested that I had a go while explaining what I was doing and aiming for - 1200 feet, 45 knots and positioned over a certain bush, tip into the dive and release at about 800 feet, pulling out before 500 feet - and not going too fast etc.

Bloggs had another go at a dummy run, but didn't improve

much. We had now wasted over 30 minutes; we had to be back in the next 30, so we *had* to start firing. Initially we fired singles, but results were appalling - off plot high and low alternately, meaning the rockets were out of sight to the personnel marking the strikes as the missile hit the ground. Bloggs had a good sweat on at this stage, very aware that he was screwing up, and that fact was also working against him. It's called 'the slippery slope' in military aviation.

OK, let's do another dummy run to settle down and then start firing pairs. We came downwind at 800 feet then on base leg the speed got up to 90 knots - oh dear. We then flew a quite nice circuit for a change, made the port and starboard armament selector and master switches live, and were ready to fire a pair. On base leg we were close to 1200 feet with the nose up to lose speed to 45 knots, when Bloggs uncovered the firing button and pressed it! The aircraft was 90 degrees off the firing heading and pointing at a village about five miles away. I saw his thumb uncover the switch and was just mouthing the words *'keep the cover on until on a firing heading'* when the noise of two rockets accelerating from rest to supersonic speed filled the air.

I took control of the aircraft and threw it around onto the firing heading, then told Bloggs to select 'ripple' and press the button again. He started saying that we weren't allowed to ripple, but my powerful and vivid expletives broke through his objections - and we got rid of all the rest in one go. Sadly I didn't have the time or state of mind to enjoy this highly illegal barrage.

I reported the incident to Range control, told them to send a truck out and we then flew round the coast in search of the damage trail I knew had to exist somewhere in that village. Luckily we found the first one very easily, a dark slash in the dry soil of a ploughed field just 50 yards (yes, it was a pre-metric incident!), short of a very imposing, large, sprawling bungalow on the cliff top, with a gardener tending each of the five acres of lawn! The village was a further mile to the left, thankfully. The ground crew dug the rocket out of the soil and discovered it was a 'twirler', ie. one of the four tail fins failed to flip out as it left its launcher tube, giving it a circular motion through the air which rather limited its flight path. The other missile must have gone right over the top of the sprawling bungalow and then fallen harmlessly into the sea, thank goodness.

Needless to say, there was a formal Ship's Inquiry, at which I thought the very least they would recommend was a Court Martial for the captain of the errant aircraft - me!

Luckily, I got nothing at all, though young Bloggs got a ship's 'logging' - or literally (and appropriately), an *official* rocket!

RED DRAGON & WINGS

Surgeon Lt Rick Jolly   **HMS Hermes**   **1975**

In February 1974, the Commando carrier HMS *Hermes* had embarked on a Western Atlantic deployment to the Caribbean and Canada. At this stage in his Naval career, HRH the Prince of Wales was a fully qualified Jungly pilot and member of 845 Squadron, now embarked in the carrier along with the Royal Marines of 42 Commando RM. After a series of exercises in Puerto Rico and some leisure time using the excellent USMC facilities at Vieques, the big carrier sailed north for the St Lawrence River, before visiting Quebec and Montréal.

'*Red Dragon*', the codename by which the Prince of Wales was known, had proved to be a popular, pleasant and effective young member of 845. Apart from having to fly an aircraft that was maintained and cosseted to Queen's Flight standards, and marked with 'Dayglo Red' fuselage panels as well, he was merely another junior pilot on the various duty rosters and flight schedules. Every now and again however, the reality of his background and future duties broke through, as when I took him diving and asked, when planning the dip, what his qualification was. HRH looked puzzled, then replied that he was President of the British Sub-Aqua Club!

One Sunday, as we headed north, the weather was hot and the sea calm. The aft end of the flight deck was cordoned off for the ship's company to indulge in a spot of 'bronzing', with the forward half cleared for flying operations involving the two aircraft of Red Dragon Flight. One *Wessex* was flown solo (with an aircrewman) by HRH himself, the other by a senior instructor. Their joint mission was to transfer underslung loads of empty beer barrels from HMS *Hermes* across to the RFA stores ship that was steaming along about two miles away on the port quarter. There, a large number of full beer barrels were awaiting the return trip.

While the ship's company sizzled in the heat, with constant reminders on the Tannoy not to be deceived by the gentle breeze cooling our skins, the two helicopters began their racetrack shuttle. HRH's pilot colleagues on the deck now sat up to watch the proceedings, and pointed out just how competent HRH was at handling the awkward loads. A net load of full beer barrels can behave very unpredictably, but his controlled flying gave no hint of this - and apparently it was no accident...

His *Wessex 5* had to come in alongside the carrier, slowing all the while, and then move across the deck before stopping, descending slightly and placing the heavy load down. It then had to lift, sashay forward, hover again, and hook up a larger but lighter load – this time made up of *empty* barrels. This was lifted, and then taken over to the port side once more before the aircraft accelerated gently into a climbing turn that took it back to the RFA.

These manoeuvres were being accomplished in a smooth and seamless way which all the pilots around me admired and very obviously respected. After another half an hour or so, the Prince of Wales' aircraft had almost caught up with that of his instructor! Everyone agreed that the boy was a good 'stick handler', although some were not quite so complimentary about his radio procedure…

That evening, the Wardroom bar opened at 6 pm as usual, but to the surprise of the usual suspects who were congregating as the shutters went up, HRH was present and looking thunderous. He had his usual dry sherry, quickly followed by another one before one of the pilots asked him if everything was OK. The *Red Dragon* did not mince his words. Apparently, he had been summoned to Commander (Air)'s cabin when he landed, and been given a serious dressing-down for 'showing off'!

The response of his listeners was most reassuring. All the young pilots roared with laughter, and told The Prince of Wales that he had now joined *their* club!

The rest of the deployment went wonderfully. HRH reached 500 hours, and grew a beard which surprised everyone when he returned to the UK that summer to take part in the Order of the Garter ceremony at Windsor Castle, followed by command of HMS *Bronington*. He also attended the final Deployment cocktail party held in HMS *Hermes* alongside in Montréal, where the guests were surprised to learn (on the following day) that Prince Charles had been present in the cleverly decorated hangar.

Had they known who, or even where he was, they might have seen one of the young pilots of 845 worm his way through the crowd and tell the Heir to the Throne that <u>if</u> the *'other job'* ever fell through, he was always welcome to come back and fly with them!

The junior Jungly disappeared into the crowd before the great and the good could grab him. Needless to say, *Red Dragon* was absolutely delighted!

JUNGLIES AT PLAY

PISSY FISHERMEN

S/Lt Mike Abbey   **845 Sqn**   **1976**

It was an age old game but must have been devised with bored Junglies in mind, whiling away off-duty moments at RAF Aldergrove during the Northern Ireland troubles. It involved poker dice and at least four players (preferably many more), all in possession of 4 glasses of some high alcohol content liqueur. Each player had to make his own choice of fluids, which was usually of four different types in order to 'spike' the opposition on either side.

The game was played by rolling the five poker dice - and after that the rules got complicated. It all depended on the addition of aces, Kings and Queens that were rolled, up to a total of five. You passed one glass to the left, or one glass to the right, or drank one glass, dependent on the fifth ace, king or queen rolled. You could also just pass on the dice to the next man if you were lucky enough not to hit a critical number. If you got to the stage where there was no liquor left in front of you it was the end of the game - and relaxation probably involved thinning down the liquor with a refreshing pint of beer.

An occasional individual would end up feeling violently ill and socially confused, much to the merriment of those who were not! The last man standing was the winner, but he then had to 'skooch' the last glass left in front of him, passing a mouthful of fluid from cheek to cheek for at least one minute, before regurgitating it into the original glass, saluting the Queen or President to ensure no cheating, and then re-consume it in one gulp, usually followed by a sharp intake of breath. Any other players remaining standing would then catch the winner before he hit the ground.

Being an impressionable young Sub Lieutenant, some older and less responsible members of the detachment (namely Lts Port, Deuxberry and Lord) persuaded me to go for the all time *skooching* record which stood at two minutes. Eager to impress my more senior colleagues, I duly took the bait and managed to keep the offending fluid, *crème de menthe*, in my mouth for a full five minutes before capitulating and collapsing.

Now comes the health warning!

When you keep mint and alcohol flushing from cheek to cheek for five minutes it does a lot of damage! When I woke up the following day, I had lost a couple of layers of mucous mebrane from the inside of my mouth, and my tongue had swollen to twice its normal size. I couldn't speak and had an enormous headache, but my breath smelt very nice indeed!

CANADIAN RODEO

Lt Nick Foster   *Joke* **Flight, 845 Sqn**   **1979**

In the less politically correct days of the 70's and 80's, it was a Jungly game when in the bar, to bite an unsuspecting female's bottom - while your oppo timed how long it was before you were 'swatted' off by the said female. For some historical reason, lost in the mists of time this evolution was known as *The Canadian Rodeo*.

Now picture the scene. It was Happy Hour at a certain RAF mess near the entrance to the Mediterranean and five Jungly pilots had disembarked from one of the LPDs for the weekend. Ale had been quaffed in significant quantities when one of the boys spied a 'chunky' woman, with her back to him, across the Mess bar. "*Get the watch on me*", says Willie H*rr*w*r, and proceeds to sneak up and bite her bottom. As usual, there was the anguished cry of surprise, which quickly turned to an indignity-fuelled fury, accompanied by frantic beating of the attacker about the head.

Our hero then returned to the Naval grouping at the end of the bar, having achieved a very respectable time. Well, this particular lady was so enraged by what had happened that she just ran at Willie with her head down – I couldn't help but be reminded of a charging bull. Willie neatly sidestepped this onrush and she careered into one of those tall bar stools (with a seat rather like a Pontefract Cake), still with her head down, which she had unfortunately got stuck between two stool legs!

She then reared up, with the stool over her head and the legs sticking out like four horns, completing the image of a furious bull. The whole Mess collapsed in gales of laughter and the offended female shook the stool off and stormed out.

The assembled Junglies thought this was a huge joke, until one of the Cr*bs pointed out that we had just seriously offended the wife of the Mess President! The bravado induced by the copious quantity of ale that we had consumed kept us (nervously) chuckling away until, sometime later, a furious-looking Wing Commander entered the Mess and demanded to see the RN Detachment Commander. That was me. As I followed him into one of the adjacent ante-rooms, I foresaw another imminent roasting, plus consequential punishments from both my Senior Pilot and the CO. With a stern frown, he asked if it was indeed someone from the Jungly detachment who had bitten his wife's bum. I owned up, but imagine my surprise when his face exploded in a broad grin! He said it was the funniest thing he had heard of in a long time, and that he would now like to buy the whole team a large round!

It was only later that we heard that the PMC and his wife were not on speaking terms, either before or after that incident!

SICILIAN TREE JUMPING

Lt Nick Foster again, still 845   **1979**

If anyone has been to Taormina in Sicily, they will recall that it's a very pretty Italian town, perched on top of cliffs some 300 feet above a small harbour and reached via a narrow, very steep and hairpinned road. In the late 70's the assault ships *Fearless* and *Intrepid* also doubled as the Dartmouth Training Squadron, teaching cadets and Sub Lieutenants on course at the Naval College all the various elements of operating a ship at sea. It was normal for two *Wessex 5s* to embark for each three month deployment and I was the Flight Commander on this particular cruise. We were anchored off Taormina when our tale begins.

Leave had been piped early in the morning and as there was a Mess dinner onboard that night, the Flight pilots were soon in a liberty boat in order to maximise the run-ashore time. The walk up the steep and winding road into town was not too far, but the incline made it quite exhausting and you can imagine the thirst we had built up on arrival. Much later, *very* much later, someone realised that time was marching on and we would have to leave right away in order to get back in time for the Mess dinner.

We duly set off, somewhat the worse for wear after many beers and much local vino. Although it was only 300 feet from top to bottom, the zigzag road meant it was a considerable distance to walk and we could see the liberty boat waiting. Lining each bend in the road were those tall narrow Mediterranean fir trees and it occurred to me (well, I was the senior officer present, and therefore allowed to have all the ideas!) that our descent would be much quicker if we jumped into the top of one of the trees near the apex of a corner, which would then bend down to the next level about 30 feet below. That way, we could step off and then repeat the process all the way down.

The rest of the Flight didn't seem so keen, and insisted on a demonstration from their brave Flight commander! Full of vino, beer and confidence, I took a good run, launched myself into midair and bear-hugged the tree just as planned. The tree then bent over as I thought it would, but as I approached the lower level, my confidence disappeared - and I failed to let go. Like a ruler being 'twanged' in a desk, the tree shuddered back into the vertical position, with me now clinging on, some 30 feet up!

Of course, those sort of firs also have all the branches pointing upwards so trying to get down and out of one (even when sober) is no mean feat. Suffice to say that by the time I did extricate myself, scratched all over and clothes ripped, the rest of the Flight had walked the long way down, howling with laughter and with absolutely no intention of attempting to emulate the same trick! One of the boys had laughed so much that he had lost a certain feature of bodily control and as a result of 'following through', had acquired a slightly awkward gait on his way down the hill, although he never openly confessed.

We did make it to the Wardroom Mess dinner eventually, but that's yet *another* story!

PIANOFORTES

Various   845/846/848/Clockwork   19??

It is not much known in the outside world that the Jungly fraternity have long had an affinity with pianos. Jungly pilots rarely played them, probably because too much skill was required, but the process of 'acquiring' and/or 'modifying' them became something of an art form, especially when 'trophy ' status had been conferred.

I forget when this story all started, but it was probably in the 1970's when HMS *Bulwark* had a very fine piano that was destroyed during a 'Saturday night at sea'. This device had the temerity to play a bum note during a wardroon sing-song, and after serious deliberation (of just a few nanoseconds) was then totally wrecked and disassembled. Within half and hour, most of its component parts had gone out through the Wardroom scuttle (the corect term for a 'porthole', and some 14 inches across) while the frame was subjected to a 'float test' from the quarterdeck, under the eyes of a very surprised lifeboat sentry.

HMS *Bulwark*'s Commander, a wonderful fellow called Ronnie Laughton, said that 848 Sqn had to replace the piano, and so we did. A really fine instrument was acquired for just in excess of a tenner, then resprayed in camouflage colours and given the callsign **'VV'**, with all the appropriate warning markings in the right places It even had its own Form *A700* (aircraft technical logbook) to record playing hours. This was presented to the Commander at a Mess dinner and he was well pleased, but unfortunately a few of the ship's officers did not spot the funny side, and aparently thought that a camouflaged piano did not go well with the chintz covers on the armchairs!

At the next ship's maintenance period they had **VV** resprayed in white, with little bits of golden moulding added afterwards. Very beautiful it was, too. When the Squadron re-embarked for the next deployment, at the first 'Saturday night at sea' it was deemed to be time to hear the 'new' piano in action, although VV was sorely missed. The playing started well, but suddenly the piano missed a note, the very note (we thought) that had been missing in **VV**! Gadzooks, was this indeed our Jungly piano, **VV,** now dressed up like a poofter? Well, you guessed it, out through the scuttle and over the guardrails she went.

Also long ago, lost in the mists of time and clouds of exhaust fumes, a detachment from 846 Sqn was doing some mountain flying training at RAF Valley in Anglesey. At the same time, a detachment of *Lightning* fighters from 11 Squadron were also present, one of whose pilots was a birthday boy. A 'sing song' was clearly in order, and so the very smart Mess piano was dragged out from under its covers, and both playing and raucous singing commenced.

Unfortunately, the piano then played a bum note, and so had to be disciplined, because after all that was the law of the land.

A little lighter fuel was poured in to loosen up the works - which unfortunately then caught fire. This may have had something to do with the fact that along with the lighter fuel, a couple of Mark 8 thunderflashes had been added to the mix. Throughout the fire and detonations, the pianist continued to play - at least until his nylon trousers started to melt! You could tell he was Air Force from that fact, because a Naval Officer would never have artificial fibres around his nether regions.

The fire became really quite spectacular, and the airfield fire engines were sent over to put out the blaze. This so reduced the fire cover on the airfield that the student *Gnat* night flying programme had to be cancelled.

It later transpired that the piano was a very fine one, borrowed for the Mess Ball and 11 Squadron had had to pay for it. They asked us for a contribution, which we presented to them in Malta a little later, where - good chaps that they were - they had already had their leave stopped for holding up score cards to mark the *Air Malta* 727's landings. This was not a good idea with Dom

Mintoff on board! Our contribution was a fiver, plus some change embedded in plastic, with the plinth made from a burnt piano key.

Even later, in Norway in the '80s, another piano was destroyed. This one belonged to 339 Squadron of the Royal Norwegian Air Force at Bardufoss Air Station; it normally lived in their crewroom, but also went into the field whenever they did.

It was the time of year for the biennial NATO exercise when every man and his dog seemed to turn up for a stab at Arctic warfare. It seemed a good idea (at the time!) to create a little diversion for the Press as well as the oh-so-serious exercise planners. However, the piano would have to be replaced, but how could we get one out from UK at short notice? The Royal Air Force would not have been amused at the request to fly one out in a *Hercules,* so the answer was to crate the piano up and label it *'Essential Engine Spares'*, which of course they were happy to carry in a C-130.

The best bit was uncrating it on the ramp of the Herc on a hardstanding 167 miles inside the Arctic Circle, and then watching the Cr*bs' faces! Anyway, the piano was decked out with *FLY NAVY* in Dayglo red, then flown under a *Sea King 4* by me and 'Twill' to be placed on the very pinnacle of the highest mountain for miles around, called Estind. Naturally it wasn't just put on the top; it did require a bit of 'sideways' thinking in order to access it. A challenge was then issued to all the competing NATO forces to get it down by any means that they could. This instantly caused the press pack to drop all the news of the exercise and concentrate on the competition!

Many air forces tried and failed to retrieve it, but eventually 339 with their *Hueys* and a team wearing ropes and crampons, armed with ice axes were winched down. They secured it in a rope sling and flew it off under a wonderful old *Huey*. They then appeared on national and international TV, playing the piano once again in their tent in the field.

The piano then had a spell as a trophy in the 339 Sqn crewroom, much to their delight and boastful pride, especially when they were visited by the Brits for a beer call. The irritation eventually became too much and in a daring night-time raid, 'our' piano was repatriated by the brave Junglies. This involved one of our number secreting himself in the loo after one such high-spirited beer call and then opening one of the cellar windows after everyone else had gone home. It then did a bit of to-ing and fro-ing between Brit and Nog crewrooms, but when J Beattie Esq came on the scene in 1983, it had been re-captured by the Noggies and then securely bolted 75 feet high up on the front of their hangar, painted rather sensibly in a very eye-catching Union Jack design!

This needed action of course and very much aware that we had elements of two squadrons and a permanent staff on site, JB contrived to form a joint Jungly and Bootneck team to retrieve it. 'Wilkie', our tame Royal Marines Mountain Leader, sent an assault group up onto the roof that abseiled down to the piano, whilst 845 Squadron's CO and JB climbed up the inside of the wall and sawed through the bolts!

Down below, the rest of the joint team waited, briefed to keep any Norwegian security staff at bay. They then received the piano when lowered down by rope, put it into a trailer, and drove it back to the Brit lines. The plan worked like a dream, even to the point of a Noggie security patrol stopping and chatting to the decoy team, whilst the hangar was alive with 'infiltrators', including a couple of 'spidermen' up on the front wall!

End of winter Exercise time, and it was essential to make some sort of impressive and spectacular move of the old Joanna. Because we were a multi-part unit, BT decided to trust the *Wessex* CO to take it into the mountains and give it to the *Sea King* CO who had found somewhere to put it where the Norwegians would be able to see, but not actually get to. This would involve a ledge around 200 feet below the lip of an overhang and swinging the piano in under a *Sea King 4*, on a very long strop at the end of the winch wire. However, we first had to display the object to the Noggies, who were in the field, as indeed were our own squadrons. The *Wessex* CO decided it was of such immense importance that he would do it personally, at which stage alarm bells should have rung quite loudly, but Beattie was let down once again by his poorly developed character judgement.

CO 845 picked up the load as planned and flew over the Norwegian tented camp, igniting coloured smoke flares attached to the piano and tossing thunderflashes out of the back of the aeroplane. This triumphalism bit went very well indeed, if a little colourful and noisy for the Noggies, who were suitably humbled to the point where they even tried to 'scramble' a *Huey* to take hot pursuit!

The naughty bit was when he got back to the 846 Squadron base, high up an icy mountain, where it all went horribly wrong. No one had briefed the 846 Squadron troops about the event and when a *Wessex 5* appeared, flying down 846 Sqn's tent line with a piano underslung, they took a bit of umbrage. However, when it stopped in the hover and blew one of the tents down, they became rather seriously annoyed, especially the chaps who lived in the tent!

Shortly thereafter CO 845 landed the piano in the snow, pickled off the strop - and disappeared over the horizon. It was at about this point when the 846 troops raced over and doused it with naptha, a high octane fuel used to power their cookers, and without further delay set light to it. All the *Sea King* Sqn CO could do thereafter was to ensure a decent burial at sea, and it was ceremoniously flown to the nearest fjord and dropped in from a great height.

Despite an iron frame and seriously charred wood, the wretched thing floated! Who knows, it may well still be a hazard to shipping somewhere up inside the waters of the Arctic Circle...

JUNGLIES ON HOME TURF

CASEVAC NORTHERN IRELAND

Lt Mike Tidd   **845 Sqn**   **1978**

Les Port, our crewman 'Chocks' Merson and I were engaged in South Armagh tasking, operating out of the wonderfully spooky old Bessbrook Mill, when we got a call to say that urgent Casualty Evacuation was needed from the base at Forkhill, at the time occupied by the Royal Green Jackets. We diverted from the task in hand and made all speed down to Forkhill, which was one of the bases right on the border with Eire. South Armagh at that time was the part of Northern Ireland known as 'Bandit Country' because it was staunchly Republican IRA territory and so dangerous for

British Forces that all movement had to be by air. Attacks on the Security Force bases at Forkhill, Crossmaglen and Newtonhamilton were very common - and also difficult to defend against. The perimeters were protected by high wire fencing to keep out the mortars and rockets, which were invariably fired from a site hidden from the defenders' view.

As we approached the Forkhill landing site, situated outside the stockade, we could see smoke drifting out from inside the fortified area. We landed on and a soldier came running to brief 'Chocks' at the cabin door; *"He says they are being mortared"* Chocks calmly relayed. *"Oooh"* said Les and he and I sat a good deal lower in our seats, in order to get down behind the Kevlar armour plates in our side doors.

Over the next few minutes a variety of casualties, ranging from walking wounded to one very badly injured chap who was brought out on a wooden door, were lifted into the back of the aircraft along with the doctor from Forkhill. Once loaded, we lifted and beat a very speedy retreat up the valley, away past Bessbrook and set off at maximum speed for the Military Wing of Musgrave Park Hospital on the southern outskirts of Belfast.

In the cabin of the Wessex, the doc was very busy stabilising the seriously injured chap - as best he could. Eventually he was able to take a break and looking round, noticed a squaddy standing at the front of the cabin with his hands casually holding on to the cabin roof. He asked him what was wrong with him and the lad replied *"I got hit in the leg, Doc"* - and then dropped his trousers to reveal a hole right through the top of his inner thigh. Obviously still in shock, and therefore not yet registering any pain, his only additional comment, on sighting this new aperture into his body was: *"Cor, that was lucky - it nearly got me family jewels!"*

I'm pleased to report that we got them all back to Musgrave Park in time and they all survived. A positive outcome made these missions the most satisfying form of tasking that we ever did. After the drop off at Musgrave Park we headed back to base at Aldergrove, with the back of the aircraft looking a bit like a butcher's shop. At that time we had WRNS maintainers from 707 training Squadron on loan - to give the girls some front-line experience. We taxied into dispersal and shut down. As the rotors stopped, one of the Wrens ran across, and before we could warn her she leapt into the back of the aircraft to get the engine intake blanks. A couple of seconds later she re-appeared, with a hand over her mouth - and then threw up all over dispersal.

We certainly didn't mock her for that!

CHRISTMAS TIME AT OMAGH

Anonymous   **845 Sqn**   **1979**

It was a fairly quiet day as far as helo tasking went; we'd done the usual 'round robin' of the locations and were now killing time in the Ops room at Omagh, chatting to the Operations Officer, who was a very pleasant and quietly spoken Major. We were discussing, of all things, Chrimbo decorations. Apparently he was having some trouble sourcing suitable trees for the three regimental messes. Couldn't just go out and buy one from the market in those days, far too dangerous!

The weather wasn't too wonderful, with low cloud, very dark and grey, and about an hour and a half to sunset, though we wouldn't actually be seeing it that night! Nevertheless, always keen to meet a challenge, we slipped into the conversation that there were just *millions* of Xmas trees out there in the woods, all over the province, so why didn't he just mount a covert raid one dark and dirty night?

'Great plan!' he casually responded - 'and what about popping out there right now in your *Iron Chicken*'?

We agreed that this was a good plan, because it's always better to be flying than sitting around. He duly armed himself with a huge axe and a 'gollock' (a long, flat jungle knife) before we got the Wessex going and took off to the South West. We flew around for a while and there certainly were millions of trees in thousands of woods, but one with the perfect landing site and correct size tree eluded us for a while. OK, so compromise was needed here, and we eventually found a small gap in a fairly large stand of trees and told the Major that this was it. He got out and we got airborne again and flew around for twenty minutes so as not to alert terrorists, policemen, woodsmen, landowners or farmers to our presence. It must have worked, because when we got back, the

49

good Major had three good-sized trees ready to bundle into the back, along with his small pack and jacket.

It was obviously warm work cutting down trees!

As I mentioned earlier, the weather was not wonderful, and with darkness coming on we quickly wound our way back to Omagh and shut down. There, one of those things you do before entering any building, almost as routine as getting up in the morning and brushing your teeth, is to stand in front of the sandpit and 'clear' your weapon, also checking your colleagues' weapons in the same way to ensure that the breech is empty and you don't subsequently shoot your own foot off accidentally!

Sadly, it was at this point that the Major realised he couldn't partake in this routine precaution, because his pistol was hanging on a tree, in a wood, some 25 minutes flying time away, where it had been placed (by him!) just in case he got rumbled and needed it in a hurry!

Needless to say we did spend quite a time telling him we couldn't *possibly* get airborne again, as the weather was too bad etc etc. However, we couldn't keep this teasing going too long - because the weather really *was* getting worse! The aircrewman and I chatted a bit about the 'needle in a haystack' ride we were about to embark on and neither of us could honestly say we knew where we were going! Of course, we did know the general direction - and set off in some haste, hoping to jog our memories as we went along.

We were in luck and somehow found the tiny hole between the trees that we had so recently vacated - and dropped the Major off again. It took him a good ten minutes of searching, but he found his gun and scrambled back into the helicopter, an extremely relieved man. We got up to about fifty feet above the trees beforebefore meeting cloud and beat a very hasty retreat back to Omagh.

Losing a weapon is a Court Martial offence, doubly embarrassing for the Unit Operations Officer and exacerbated by the fact that he was stealing someone else's trees at the time. This could have seriously affected his career plans, but he was now one very 'Happy Hector' instead, and someone who had his present from Santa rather early that year.

WINE DELIVERY

Lt Hugh Deuxberry   **845 Sqn**   **1980**

Everything that the military used in South Armagh had to travel by air, as road travel was far too dangerous because of the success of the Provisional IRA at attacking or booby-trapping vehicles in the area. The old Mill at Bessbrook was the main security Forces base in South Armagh, through which all supplies flowed for the outlying bases at Forkhill, Crossmaglen and Newtonhamilton.

We Junglies had a four aircraft detachment supporting the Army in Northern Ireland, alongside a RAF detachment, and took regular turns at providing an aircraft for the 24-hour cover at Bessbrook. We were firm believers that flying low and fast was the best defence against small arms fire and *SAM 7* shoulder-launched missiles, which was what the PIRA were armed with at that time. As well as being a good tactic, it was also good fun flying!

The resident South Armagh unit was the Royal Green Jackets whose officers, like those of any 'proper' Army regiment who had been around for a while, drank really good wine that had been laid down by previous generations and constantly replaced with fresh stocks for the future. The company manning the Police station at Newtonhamilton were obviously finding it thirsty work and called forward an underslung load of supplies including beer, champagne and the regiment's finest claret. I should at this point explain that Newtonhamilton was an unusual security force base in that the helicopter pad was a short distance away from the fortified police station and monitored by CCTV cameras. Remaining on the ground to off-load stores from a helicopter was tantamount to giving the enemy a sitting target, so bringing in supplies by underslung load was the norm.

Anyway, young Hugh Deuxberry was tasked to take the underslung load across to Newtonhamilton. Keen as mustard, he got airborne, hooked up the load and set off westwards. In his keenness to remain tactical however, and possibly a mite forgetful, he flew a bit lower than was really advisable when carrying an underslung load and managed to drive the load through the upper branches of a tree. Not realising this, he arrived at Newtonhamilton and lowered the load carefully on to the helipad at which point his aircrewman, who was leaning out the cabin door, said: *" I think we ought to pickle it off and get out of here quick boss, before the natives get angry..."*

The reason for this very sage advice became quickly obvious as the aircraft moved sideways and the released load became visible, complete with a broken tree branch stuck into the side of it - and a large red stain spreading across the surface of the helipad in full view of the CCTV camera!

Needless to say, the boys quickly made themselves scarce but, by the time they landed back to Bessbrook, the phones were red hot and Hugh was really deep in the guano!

VCPs

Lt Pete Manley   **845 Sqn**   **1980**

The bulk of Northern Ireland flying was pretty dull and repetitive but occasionally interspersed with much excitement. In this tale, I'm afraid to say, it was all down to the self-administered aftermath of too much social!

Paul and I were tasked for an early morning two hour Vehicle Check Point (VCP) sortie. You take a ten man 'stick', drop five of them beside a road, where they stop and search any passing vehicles, whilst we proceed to drop the other five elsewhere, then come back for the first and so on, leapfrogging all over a preplanned area. On the ground at the VCP, two men position themselves at each end 50 yards out, and one in the middle with a radio; all three are hidden in the bushes.

The other two stop the target car, one covering the other. Car number plates can be checked over the radio and a thorough search made. This is intended to limit the ease with which terrorists can move arms or explosives around the Province. If there is a chance they will be stopped on the road, they may well think twice about using a road vehicle, or at least that is the theory.

Any positive contact or breakout is followed up with both sections until we have a result. This particular morning, we were both suffering from trying the Mess barman's homemade *poteen*, which is an absolutely lethal fluid - but you don't know that at the time, listening to him singing its virtues in his easy Irish brogue...

After dropping the first stick, I noticed a milk float and got the crewman to brief the second stick commander to VCP the milk float and bring me back two pints. On landing beside the float, the milkman was very surprised and not a little nervous as he handed over the two bottles – paid for, I hasten to add! Paul and I consumed them with gusto but I found the experience did not have the effect I was hoping for, as the milk didn't agree with me at all and my stomach began to misbehave. After landing at the next drop-off point I climbed down and threw up beside the wheel, in full view of the now rather concerned stick of troops. They didn't seem too happy that their pilot wasn't very well and had a worrying time wondering if we were coming back for them!

However, I felt a whole heap better after ridding myself of the offending stomach contents, and after the next pickup spotted the same float and VCP'd him again to give back the empties! The message then got out into the world of milk that there was a mad, bearded Englishman around, shopping for milk from a helicopter! Lord knows what the Army thought, but I subsequently found they were always requesting my services to cover their more awkward sorties – possibly something to do with 'rules' and my general ignorance thereof...

ARMY EXCHANGE OFFICERS

Lt Andy Jeffrey   **848 Sqn**   **1980's**

Adrian Short was a deaf-as-a-post Army Gunner, who had transferred to the Army Air Corps and was (at the time of this dit) on exchange with 848 Squadron, flying as a fully fledged Jungly. One day in Northern Ireland he was airborne from Bessbrook back to Aldergrove with a brand new, straight-out-of-training, sprog pilot in the left hand seat; the chap was eager as hell to impress, yet barely spoke for the first twenty minutes. Sprog was struggling to keep up with where they were and after finally working out how to hold the map the right way up, he called out gleefully '*Portadown*' as he finally identified the small town over which they were flying.

The poor old crewman in the back of the *Wessex* spilt his coffee everywhere as Adrian dumped the cab into autorotation and a high descent rate spiral dive. Apparently, he feared the worst, convinced by the unusual outburst from the sprog co-pilot yelling *'put her down'*, that someone must have been shooting at them!

Pete Taylor, another 'pongo' on exchange, led a plucky detachment to the Channel Islands from 845 Squadron in support of one of the school cadet forces out there. The culmination of the visit, on the last night, was a riotous party in desperate need of music. As the only known instrument anywhere near was a piano in the hospital, it fell to the Detachment Commander and an alcohol fuelled sense of duty to go and fetch it.

Unfortunately, a very senior nursing person did not appreciate the jungly assault on her hospital at some ungodly hour and remonstrated long and loud about this. No-one is quite sure how Pete did it, except him perhaps, but he eventually left with the piano and the party was even more of a roaring success than it had been previously!

A couple of days later and by now back at Yeovilton, the Senior Pilot was away and Pete Taylor (as the most senior officer around) was standing in, naturally occupying SP's office, when the phone rang. Answering as 'Senior Pilot' there ensued, listened to intently by those also in the office, long periods of silence punctuated with occasional comments such as: *"How awful"*; *"I really must apologise for such terrible behaviour"*; *"I will of course ensure that he is punished appropriately"*, and *"Would a cheque from his personal account be an appropriate gesture of compensation?"*

What luck to be the recipient of the call that should have led to a whole load of trouble! The Senor Pilot and other Squadron heavies never did find out - until now of course!

BUMP STARTED WESSEX

Lt Mike Tidd   **845 Sqn**   **1981**

In Northern Ireland, down at Bessbrook Mill, it was a lazy afternoon. We were on instant readiness with the QRF (Quick Reaction Force) troops, awaiting a call - and rather bored! Our tasker, known by everyone as 'Buzzard', asked our *Wessex* crew to take bread and papers to Fork Hill. No problem - just a pleasure to help and actually be doing something. Brief QRF they'll have to come with us in case of a call. Hmm, see a chance for some fun on the way...

During port engine start, set selector switch to 'OFF' halfway through the sequence, causing engine to run down. Repeat process for the benefit of the QRF audience. Climb out and tell the QRF that battery is a bit low, and ask for a push. Twelve soldiers manoeuvre aircraft on the pan until we can get a good run towards the boundary fence.

Sceptical QRF start to push, half-heartedly. As we roll, a couple of taps on the brakes, accompanied by pressing start button. Engine runs up, but then we abort sequence again. Slightly less sceptical QRF push aircraft back and try again. QRF now fairly convinced this *can* work, and push aircraft as far back up the ramp towards Buzzard's hut as the narrow gap will allow, no mean effort in itself. This time, with the aid of the slope and a committed QRF, the beast starts up and we have a bunch of better educated Pongos. Not one of them realised that there was no way in the world that the wheels could be connected to the whirly bits above them!

TAIL ROTOR FAILURE

Lt Phil Doyne-Ditmas   **845 Sqn**   **1981**

It was a warm, sunny day in the summer of 1981 and two 845 Squadron *Wessex* 5s from HMS *Hermes* were making their way at an impressive 90 knots up the eastern seaboard of the United States, a couple of miles out to sea. They were in transit from the naval air station at Jacksonville to the Marine Corps base at Camp Lejeune. It was a very normal detachment sortie, with a single pilot, an aircrewman (Cpl Gus Tyrell), a Chief Petty Officer maintainer in the left-hand seat and the Squadron Deputy Air Engineering Officer (Lt Pat Lynch) plus half a dozen maintenance crew in the back – and of course the baggage. This was pretty much what you would expect in terms of personal kit, with the addition of golf clubs and a bag with £2000 which comprised the Detachment's 'contingency' fund. A couple of last-minute items were chucked in too, like Divisional Documents, Flying Log Books (not many hours in mine), emergency chocolate and so on.

Lt Mike Tidd was in the lead aircraft, and we were intent on enjoying the next few weeks on exercise with the USMC. However, an hour or so into the flight, the world of those in my aircraft, XT448, changed very suddenly. A loud bang from the rear of the cab, accompanied by a severe yaw to the right, began what was to be a very interesting few minutes. Shouting at the aircrewman to tell me what was going on back aft, I automatically entered autorotation, simply because I felt that I wanted to enter a known configuration from one that was distinctly unknown to me. No simulator procedure for this one, I thought - collective lever fully down, get into autorotation, turn into wind, wherever that is (but not much of it anyway), trim the speed, try and analyse what's gone wrong...

Laconically from the back, Gus eventually came to life through the headset: "*I think we've lost a bit of the tail rotor, Boss - I can actually see one blade falling away!*". Many choice expletives followed from the front seat in my attempts both to critically appraise myself of the deep trouble we were in, as well as pass on the gist of the problem to Gus! We had never practiced anything like this in training and here I was having to make all the decisions cold.

Now down to 700 feet, I realised that this was either going to turn out at best 'average' or at worst, *very* badly. With a tail rotor failure, and we seemed to have lost all use of this device, you either take away the reason for its existence, namely the torque reaction between engines and airframe, or else keep the airspeed high enough to allow air flow along the fuselage to create a weathercock effect that keeps you flying in the right general direction, albeit sideways. The former choice was invariably preferred!

Decision time. Was it to be an engine-off landing into the water? Or a high speed run on, at an as yet unspecified airfield and at an as yet unresearched speed? The book said you first had to find the lowest sustainable speed, by trial and error, by doing a low speed handling check at altitude, but this would not be less than 70 knots.

The rate of descent was building horribly as we passed through 500 feet. Pushing the nose forward slightly to keep the speed up and the tail where it should be, I pulled in an armful of collective to further diagnose the problem. This time, there was a severe yaw the other way. This left me in no doubt that tail rotor control for the remainder of this flight was not a realistic expectation!

It was then an easy decision to make, actually, because we were still at some height, the sea was warm, and we were only a few miles offshore. Also, it was still daylight and we were both facing into a light wind and had another aircraft with us to pick up the pieces. The alternative was to fly sideways to the nearest airfield, estimated at some 40 miles away, and run on there at a speed that the *Wessex* wasn't designed for, possibly leading to a rollover - with resultant bits flying everywhere and a serious possibility of fire.

However, familiar though I was with autorotation *with* a functioning tail rotor, this was bound to be a bit different. Would the aircraft spin when I eventually pulled up on the collective at sea level? As I ran through the double engine shut-down procedure, closing the speed select levers and fuel cocks, I noticed a fairly startled expression from my cockpit companion - who was by now convinced he was in the hands of a lunatic, not having the foggiest idea what was going on.

It then went pretty quiet as the engines wound down, apart from considerable confusion in the back as the passengers sorted themselves out for a swim. You don't normally hear anything from the back above the roar and whine of running machinery, so this was mildly surreal. There was just a spare second or three to transmit a brief *Mayday* call to Leader, who by then had realised that his formation was no longer a formation.

Through the 200 foot 'gate' we plummeted and with the lever firmly held down by my rigid arm lock, I started the longest flare ever recorded, in my opinion at least. In this latter stage there was no point looking at the meaningless dials, so I concentrated instead on reducing the forward speed and rate of descent smoothly - to arrive at a point where they were both 'zero' at the same time and the wheels just about in the water. I remember thinking that the Rotor RPM was extremely 'generous' which was fantastic, and all for the better as 'money in the bank' when I came to trade this RRPM for 'lift' in the last few seconds of flight.

We finally entered the water, tail low, which to my relief

stopped any aircraft rotation as I pulled up the collective to cushion the impact as we splashed down. I squeezed the final revs from the rotors to try and keep the aircraft upright, but as these decayed and we settled into the water, two things happened very quickly.

First,the *Wessex* rolled rapidly to port, because only the starboard flotation bag inflated. Second, as the main rotor blades hit the water, everything stopped dead instantly, save for our inexorable roll to port - and under the water.

Busy trying to hold everything steady as the main rotors came to an abrupt stop, I noticed that my left seat passenger was now up to his neck in water, had unstrapped and was making his way up towards me, intent on using *my* window just before I did! Quite naturally, I pulled rank and shouted for him to wait! Jettisoning my window, I then scrambled out, followed by a very relieved passenger. By now the aircraft had rolled past 90 degrees, was virtually inverted and only just floating. The aircrewman and passengers were still clambering and swimming out of the back (luckily the cargo door was on the right side, i.e. uppermost) and we formed a loose, if slightly shocked group as we all inflated life jackets and waited for rescue by the Leader.

We took stock. We had no injuries, and no kit, but were alive - and in warm water. Then someone mentioned the possibility of sharks, which quite successfully concentrated our attention and the group gripped together a little tighter!

What remains with me from that day? A photograph of XT448 shortly before she sank, with the tail clearly visible and the complete tail rotor assembly, including the gearbox, missing. The out-of-balance forces caused by one blade flying off are huge and despite the ruggedness of the *Wessex's* construction, this was only to be expected. The photo also showed pieces of A4 size paper floating around the aircraft, which would have been the Divisional Documents hastily thrown in at the last moment – along with my Flying Log Book.

Most of all, I recall an overwhelming sense of relief that it was the *port* flotation bag that had chosen to fail, not the starboard one, and that the bonding on one of the tail rotor blades had chosen to fail when it did, rather than in a low hover, one dark and stormy night over the North Atlantic.

Postscript: *The cause of the accident was a bonding failure between the main spar and aerofoil section of one of the tail rotor blades, leading to total disintegration of the tail rotor assembly within seconds. No one ever told me that the blades were just glued together! The root cause of the port flotation bag failure was a direct consequence of a component life extension policy which (with hindsight) was rather unwise. Despite the successful controlled crash, if that failure alone had occurred on the starboard side, it could have cost several lives that day. All that remains now of XT448 is the tail light, cut away by Mike Tidd from the aircraft lying on the sea bed a few days later. Oh yes, and we never did find the £2,000 Contingency fund!*

JUNGLIES IN THE SOUTH ATLANTIC

SOUTH GEORGIA 2 – 845 SQN 0

Lt Mike Tidd   **845 Sqn**   **1982**

South Georgia, a crescent-shaped island, 105 miles long and 18.5 miles wide, rises sheer out of the sea to a height of between 7500 and 9500 ft along its spine. Over half its land mass is permanently covered by ice, in the form of glaciers. It lies in the South Atlantic on the edge of Antarctica, at virtually the same latitude as Cape Horn, and bears the full brunt of the wild weather that sweeps around the Cape. *Operation Parquet* (or *'Paraquat'* as it was unwittingly dubbed by all involved!) was the codename given to the   retaking of South Georgia in April 1982, as a prelude to *Op Corporate* and the start of the Falklands campaign.

Tucked away on the edge of Antarctica, few people had heard of it. Certainly none of 845 Naval Air Squadron 'C' Flight would have claimed to have been able to point it out in an atlas before we embarked in the fleet tanker RFA *Tidespring* at Ascension Island, to to join the Task Group which had been charged with its recapture. 'C' Flight consisted of two *Wessex 5*'s and about thirty personnel, with me as Flight Commander, Flt Lt Andy 'Pullthrough' Pulford RAF, our tame Cr*b, as my second in command, Lt Ian Georgeson, Sub Lt Andy 'Boy' Berryman, and Leading Aircrewmen Tug Wilson and Jan Lomas.   Our two aircraft, Yankee Alpha (XT473) and Yankee Foxtrot (XT464) were standard *Wessex 5's*, but fitted with SS11/AS12 rocket rails and M260 missile sights, as it was envisaged that we might be required to provide the Royal Marines with fire support against bunkers or other strongpoints at some point during the operation.

The Task Group was led by the County class destroyer, HMS *Antrim*, 'D' Squadron SAS embarked; RFA *Tidespring*, 'M' Company of 42 Commando Royal Marines embarked, and HMS *Plymouth*, a Type 12 frigate, with elements of the Royal Marines' Special Boat Squadron (SBS). The senior aviator of the group was *Antrim's* flight commander, Lieutenant Commander Ian Stanley, a very experienced 'pinger' pilot. His *Wessex 3*, known to all as 'Humphrey', was quite an old airframe but, equipped with radar and a fairly sophisticated Automatic Flight Control System (AFCS), was well suited to the task of acting as a pathfinder for our *Wessex* 5s.

On the way south *'The Red Plum'* (HMS *Endurance*) joined up with us and we received detailed briefings from Tony Ellerbeck, her Flight Commander, and David Ives, the senior hydrographer, on the terrain and the sort of weather conditions that we would find there. Having trained in Northern Norway, we were used to operating in Arctic conditions, but even so the sheer violence and unpredictability of the weather that Tony described sounded rather unpleasant, to say the least. In spite of Tony's eloquence however, I don't think that any of us realised just *how* unpleasant until we experienced the real thing at first hand. I suppose, looking back, we mentally equated the conditions that he described with the worst of the weather that we had been used to in the Arctic. As it turned out this was a bit like equating a tabbycat to a tiger!

The first phase of the operation was to carry out a detailed reconnaissance of the Argentine positions. Our mission, code-named *'Dandelion'*, was to insert Captain John Hamilton's SAS patrol 2500 feet up on Fortuna Glacier, from where they planned to make their way along the spine of the island to a point from which they could observe the Argentine garrison at Leith. Our lack of a realistic appreciation of the conditions is borne out by the fact that the initial thoughts were to use a night formation approach and a covert insertion of the SAS team onto the glacier. The *Wessex 5's* were fitted with beta lights to aid night formation flying and we even hatched a plan to do an airborne join up with Antrim's *Wessex*

3, which would lead us in using its radar!

We practised the airborne join-up with the two *Wessex 5*'s on the night of 15 April - and succeeded in frightening ourselves fartless. As 'Boy' Berryman hadn't done any night formation before, I had decided to put him in the right-hand seat and to demonstrate from the left. The process of an airborne link-up was tricky under the best of conditions, but peering round an M260 missile sight and eventually flying with my head half out of the cockpit window in air temperatures of several degrees below zero made it a very sporting business indeed!

Eventually we decided that discretion was the better part of valour, and opted for a daylight insertion. We arrived off the north-west tip of South Georgia on the morning of April 21, and after Ian Stanley had carried out an initial recce in *Humphrey*, we embarked the troops and got airborne in a three ship echelon, setting off through driving snow showers towards the coast. In accordance with normal Jungly operating procedures, our two Wessex 5's flew with a single pilot and aircrewman. I was in Yankee Alpha with Tug Wilson, and 'Pullthrough' in Yankee Foxtrot with Jan Lomas. Our first sight of the coast at Cape Constance was pretty awe-inspiring as its black cliffs rose a thousand feet vertically from the sea and appeared through the driving snow. We skirted round through the low ground at the landward end of Cape Constance and emerged into Antarctic Bay, where the foot of the Fortuna Glacier disgorges into the sea.

The turbulence was impressive - we could be using full power just to maintain height one moment, then be in full autorotation (no power applied) and still going up the next. The weather on the glacier was wall-to-wall snow; after orbiting in Antarctic Bay for some time, Ian Stanley made the decision to return to the ships and refuel. We headed back through heavy snow storms, Ian to *Antrim* and Pullthrough and I to *Tidespring*. However, *Tidespring's* deck could only operate one aircraft at a time, so I landed first, shut down and watched while CPO Raines' team quickly folded the aircraft and stowed it in the hangar. In the meantime Pullthrough was hovering off the port quarter with his aircraft building up an impressive accumulation of snow and ice...

At 1145 we tried again. This time we were able to make better progress, and climbed up on to the upper slopes of the glacier, though it was still very murky and there was severe turbulence and a lot of snow being whipped up from the surface by the wind. To add to our deep joy and happiness, we could see that the surface of the glacier was heavily crevassed, which meant that, whilst we might gain some visual references from the surface once we got close enough, we would have to be very careful about where we put down.

Ian Stanley led us up to near the top of the glacier and then turned into wind and made his approach using his Doppler and Automatic AFCS to let himself down onto the snow. As I turned into wind I realised how few visual references were going to be available to me, particularly as the last 200 feet of the approach was partially obscured by flying snow and the standard snow-landing approach would not be feasible. I overshot and went round again while my aircrewman and I discussed the problem. On the second approach I kept the aircraft orientated as best I could using the few distant references available, while Tug did a sterling job of talking me down gradually to the surface.

It was a really challenging approach to say the least. Apart from the lack of visual references, we were on the updraughting slope of the mountain and had to go into virtually full autorotation to persuade the aircraft to descend. Once close to the surface, we could see that the crevassing was even worse than originally imagined. We eventually touched down with a crevasse about ten feet away on our starboard side and started off-loading the troops. Despite having the collective lever fully down (no power applied), I found that we were being moved sideways and backwards by the wind. Even sat on the surface we still had 60 knots of airspeed on the clock and I ended up having to fly the aircraft to try and keep it in position while Tug off-loaded everyone and everything as quickly as possible - before we slid into the adjacent crevasse.

As soon as the off-load was complete, we bounded into the air and scuttled off down the glacier and back into Antarctic Bay to wait for the others - before breathing a huge sigh of relief and returning to the ships. Back on board *Tidespring*, 'Pullthrough' and I debriefed, agreeing that we had never flown in conditions like these before, and said: "*Thank Christ we'll never have to do anything like that ever again!*"

How wrong can you be?

Overnight, we were meant to keep one aircraft on Casevac (Casualty Evacuation) standby, but as night came the barometer dropped 30 millibars in an hour and the wind rose to peak gusts of 80 knots. The weather changed so fast that we were unable to fold the rotors on the deck alert aircraft, and its restraining tipsocks, which were meant to anchor the tips of the rotor blades and prevent them thrashing up and down in the wind, started to tear themselves apart. In the end we anchored the blades with heavy manila mooring lines, lashed everything else down to the best of our ability and then wedged ourselves into our bunks to get what rest we could overnight.

When morning came and the wind eased down to just a full-blown gale we were quite surprised to find that the aircraft was still in one piece. However, up on Fortuna Glacier things were not looking so good. Overnight the wind on the glacier had peaked at over 100 knots and John Hamilton's team had had their shelters torn away. They were now cold, wet and starting to become hypothermic. We were not all that surprised when, at 10 00, they called for urgent evacuation as they were suffering from frostbite and exposure. Our planned duty roster would have put Ian Georgeson and Andy Berryman in the frame to fly. However, though I was quite happy that Ian (the world's most unflappable and likeable Scot) was experienced enough for the task, the 'Boy', though a very competent young pilot, was still too new to the game to operate in the sort of conditions that 'Pullthrough' and I had experienced the day before.

In addition I felt that someone with previous knowledge of the conditions and the lie of the land should go. I could hardly 'joe' Pullthrough to do something that I didn't want to do myself, so I put myself down to fly Yankee Foxtrot with Tug Wilson and Ian with Jan Lomas in Yankee Alpha. It would be fair to say that neither of us was looking forward to the trip but, if I had to go up there again, I was glad to have Tug with me. He and I knew each other from our time flying Wasps and I had great respect for his calm reliability and unfailing sense of humour.

We launched between snowstorms at about 10 30 and headed inshore. As we entered Antarctic Bay the weather over the glacier looked pretty awful, so Ian Stanley ordered our two *Wessex* 5's to land on the low ground at Possession Bay while he recce'd ahead. Ian Georgeson, in his inimitable fashion, soon had Jan Lomas out wading about in the snow, taking happy snaps of all of us with Ian's camera.

Eventually Ian Stanley returned to say that he had been unable to find a break in the weather over the glacier and so we returned to the ships to refuel and wait. An hour or so later we tried again, and this time arrived at the foot of the glacier - to find a break in the cloud. As we set off up the glacier we were acutely aware that, unusually, we were going to be very short of escape options up there. In this case, if we got caught in the air by the weather, we might be unable to land because of whiteout, and also unable to climb as we were already experiencing icing. The only route in or out was the one we were taking, as we had mountains on either side of us and in the *Wessex 5* we had no radar, Doppler or Automatic Flight Control System.

Ian Stanley led us up through the clear patch and as we approached the top of the glacier, spotted the smoke grenades that the SAS team had fired to mark their position. They had only moved a few hundred yards from where we had dropped them, and were now huddled together in the lee of some rocks in an area that was relatively free of crevasses. Their smoke grenades had stained the snow around them, making the approach and landing relatively straightforward this time. We landed facing our escape route down the glacier, which at this point was a fairly shallow ice slope leading down about a mile to a ridge, on the other side of which the ice dropped away much more steeply.

Tug got weaving down the back and soon had our stick of tired half-frozen troops loaded. As soon as they were all onboard he shut the door and broke out some hot soup that he had brought along - to get some warmth back into them. Meanwhile I had radioed Ian Stanley and asked to depart, as I could see a fresh belt of cloud and snow brewing up near our escape route. As soon as I got the OK I lifted and headed off down the valley at about 60 knots and 100 ft, which should have given me the opportunity to attempt landing on again if the weather got too bad. As it was, the speed with which South Georgia weather changes proved too quick for me. About half a mile along the valley, the wind suddenly shifted, and without warning I was in complete whiteout and in thick, driving snow.

The effect of whiteout is very difficult to describe adequately to anyone who has not experienced it. Basically, the flying snow over a white and featureless background obscures all visual references - and leaves you totally disorientated. If this happens to you on skis it can be quite frightening, but when you are airborne over a glacier, with 'cumulo-granite' mountains on either side and no ability to climb up out of trouble, it was all very bad news indeed! The only option that remained was to try and get the aircraft back down on to the ground - if I could just find a reference to land by. I had passed a small clump of rocks a few seconds earlier, so I called down to Tug to let him know that we had a problem and then banked to the left - a 50/50 decision that probably (inadvertently) saved all our lives.

Tug threw open the cabin door and leaned out to look for the surface as I tried to turn and regain a landing reference. Unfortunately, what neither of us could see was that we were in a dip in the ice and as I glanced in at the instruments halfway round the turn, I saw the radalt (radar altimeter) winding down at an alarming rate. I had no idea where the ground had suddenly come from but, realising that a collision was inevitable, I pulled in power and flared the nose up to cushion the impact. The aircraft hit the ground left wing low and tail first, doing about 30 knots, shearing the port undercarriage leg off and crashing down onto its left side.

I remember lying in my seat harness with a feeling of intense frustration, watching the left-hand side of the cockpit filling up with debris and snow and thinking '*Mrs Tidd isn't going to like being a widow*!' Eventually the aircraft ground to a halt. Inertially operated 'crash' switches in the nose had stopped the engines and apart from the wind and my windscreen wiper, which was still squeaking away, it was relatively quiet. I reached down beside me to turn off the fuel cocks and electrics, only to find that the whole lot was buried under snow and broken glass.

Tug called through from the cabin that everyone seemed to be in one piece, so I hauled open the starboard cockpit window, climbed up onto the side of the fuselage and helped Tug get the cabin door fully open. By this time the other two aircraft had arrived and were able to use the wreckage of my helo as a visual reference to land by. I staggered across to the cabin door of Ian Stanley's *Wessex 3* and plugged myself into the intercom lead that

Fitz, his aircrewman, handed me. Ian's first words were: "*You messy bastard, you've left your windscreen wiper on!*" to which I replied with some feeling: "*If you're so f***ing clever you go and turn it off!*"

Fitz bounded off into the snow and with the help of Tug and Jan Lomas, divided up our survivors between *Humphrey* and Ian Georgeson's *Wessex 5*, which was busy jettisoning fuel to bring the aircraft weight down so that it could lift the extra load. Once all survivors had been loaded, the two aircraft waited for a break in the weather and then lifted off in formation, heading off down the glacier. By this time the press of bodies in the back of the *Wessex 3* had forced me to unplug from the intercom to make room and I must have been lost in my own thoughts. I don't remember much about the flight back to the ships, until we landed on *Antrim*.

Once onboard, I climbed out, gave Ian Stanley a thumbs up in thanks and made my way across the Flight Deck into the hangar. Inside, First Aid parties were busy laying out stretchers, making up saline drips and very obviously preparing to receive casualties. Why? I took my bone-dome off, grabbed hold of Chief Heritier, Ian Stanley's Senior Maintenance Rating, and told him that it was all OK! He could relax - our only casualty had suffered nothing worse than a cut cheek. He looked at me for a moment and then took me by the arm and said: "*You obviously haven't heard, sir. The other Wessex 5 crashed into a cliff on the way out. We don't know yet if there are any survivors*".

The shock hit me like a blow to the guts and for a moment I felt physically sick. Jock Georgeson, Jan Lomas and Tug were good friends of mine - and to hear that they were probably dead, on top of what I had just been through left me feeling cold, dazed and weak. I then heard *Humphrey* lifting off again, and in something of a daze was taken up to debrief Brian Young, *Antrim's* captain and the Task Group Commander. He had been a tough Fleet Air Arm jet pilot in his time, but considering that he had just seen the whole operation come off the rails and blow up in his face, he was very sympathetic. I think Ian Stanley must have talked to him about the conditions on the glacier the day before, because when I told him how we had been overwhelmed by the speed with which the weather changed, he seemed to understand - and told me not to blame myself.

I was led away to the wardroom and given a hot drink

while we waited for news. I don't think I registered much more until the Ops Room announced that *Humphrey*'s crew had made contact with Yankee Alpha's crew and that they had *all* survived! I cannot adequately describe the relief that I felt when I heard this. It was some time later before Ian Stanley managed to find a hole in the weather to get in and pick up Ian Georgeson. The story of that remarkable piece of flying is best left to Ian Stanley and his crew to describe.

Suffice to say that he and his crew managed to pack sixteen armed men into an aircraft cabin that normally feels cramped with four people in it. They then flew back through horrible weather and managed to land on a heaving deck at well above his normal Maximum All Up Weight. Ian was later appointed to the Distinguished Service Order (*DSO)* and in my opinion it was richly deserved (even if he was a 'pinger'!)

Once Ian Georgeson was dried off, we sat down to debrief and he filled me in on what had happened. Having embarked the survivors from my aircraft, they had started off down the glacier through a break in the weather with the *Wessex 3* in the lead. Within half a mile however, the weather had closed in again and they were in whiteout. The *Wessex 3* with its radar and FCS was able to continue using its automatic height-hold to maintain height over the surface, and initially Ian had been able to formate on it. Unfortunately, what neither crew could see was that they were approaching a ridge of ice, and as *Humphrey*'s height-hold caused it to descend on the far side of the ridge, Ian Georgeson suddenly found himself having to descend to try and hold on to his formation position, only to find his radalt winding down fast to indicate that the surface was coming up to meet him.

He pulled in power to cushion the landing, and probably would have got away with it if the wind had not been blowing at 40-50 knots from the side. He touched down hard and the aircraft rolled over because it was still moving sideways. Stewart Cooper, the co-pilot in the *Wessex 3,* had mistaken the cloud of snow that was thrown up as the blades hit the ground for the *Wessex 5* running headlong into a cliff! Luckily no-one was hurt, with the exception of the same SAS sergeant who already had a cut on his cheek when he was struck by the machine gun (GPMG) in the crash in my aircraft, who now received a matching cut a couple of inches further down his cheek from the GPMG in Ian's!

Jan Lomas soon had the troops mustered out on the ice and after persuading them to be in a photo of the crew sitting on their wrecked aircraft (only Jock Georgeson would have thought of that!), inflated the aircraft dinghy and got everyone in out of the weather. For the next few hours they kept everyone occupied playing cards until Ian Stanley's crew finally managed to reach them - and rescue them too.

The loss of two-thirds of the Task Group's troop-carrying helicopter assets was a major blow to the operational plan but, as it turned out, not a fatal one. HMS *Brilliant*, a Type 22 frigate with two *Lynx* helicopters embarked, was diverted from the main Falklands Task Force to reinforce the South Georgia Task Group.

Four days later, after several more trials and tribulations which are a fascinating tale in their own right, *Humphrey*, despite being one of the Fleet Air Arm's oldest helicopters, successfully attacked the Argentine *Guppy* class submarine *Santa Fe* with Mk11 depth charges, probably the oldest airborne weapon in the Navy's inventory. As the damaged *Santa Fe* limped back into Grytviken, she was harried by HMS *Endurance's Wasp* firing AS12 missiles which, though they did little damage as they passed through the glassfibre fin without exploding, completely demoralised the submarine's crew, particularly when one of the missiles neatly removed the leg of a Petty Officer who was climbing the ladder inside the fin.

Tidespring, with the main body of troops embarked, was over 100 miles away at this point. The moment was too good to waste however, so the military HQ staff, *Antrim*'s own Royal Marine detachment and the SAS were quickly formed into an assault group and flown ashore by *Humphrey* and *Brilliant*'s two aircraft. Ian Georgeson and I manned the Military Ops Room in *Antrim* as she and *Plymouth* steamed in at high speed to provide NGS (Naval Gunfire Support).

I stepped out onto the upper deck for a moment on the way in to the gunline and will never forget the sight of the two long grey hulls, their Battle Ensigns flying as they raced through heavy seas with the barrels of their 4.5" guns lifting and training towards the shore. It was a sight that had probably not been seen since the Second World War.

The warships then laid down a barrage of high explosive around the Argentine positions in order to keep their heads down and demoralise them, rather than to do any physical damage, as it was vital to keep the British Antarctic Survey buildings intact. The troops were ferried ashore to Hestesletten on the other side of Grytviken inlet, from where they advanced through Grytviken itself to attack the Argentine positions at King Edward Point. Thoroughly demoralised, the Argentines soon surrendered and by early evening Brian Young was able to send this historic signal: *'Be pleased to inform Her Majesty that the White Ensign flies alongside the Union Flag at Grytviken, South Georgia. God save the Queen'.*

Despite some major setbacks, the first phase of the operation to recover the Falkland Islands had been successfully completed...

SALTY ENGINE FAILURE

Lt Cdr David Baston   848 Sqn   Apr 1982

I was one of the 848 Sqn aircrew being ferried south to the Falkland Islands in the Cunard freighter *Atlantic Conveyor*, armed with *Wessex 5*s and a quartet of RAF *Chinooks*. The *Wessex 5* played a major role in support to the motley fleet scraped together to make up the Task Force, including doing the Helicopter Delivery Service (HDS) role - or whatever else was required.

One very stormy day, the Task Force commander decided to hold a conference for all Captains and Masters of the assembled fleet and off we went to the merchantmen to pick up and deliver them, winching up one by one from their vessels, most of which of course didn't have helidecks. I had about six of them in the back and was in the middle of winching up Captain John Morton, the Master of the MV *Elk* (an ammunition ship), when a huge rogue wave came over her bows and hit us full frontal.

The next few moments really concentrated my attention as the starboard engine 'ran away up' and the port engine stopped. Now, a 'runaway up' means that the engine goes to above design maximum RPM and takes the rotor RPM with it. In the *Wessex 5* the single engine performance was rather impressive, and this was very fortuitous as it still gave full power, allowing me to fly away from the ship - whilst recovering the Master, who throughout the incident was hanging on the winch wire!

It now seemed a good moment to restart the port engine, hoping that all the seawater had drained out of it. Just as Rolls-Royce intended, it started as though nothing had happened - and so I advanced the speed select lever to let it join in the fun. The starboard engine meanwhile was giving its all and I was somewhat concerned that it would blow up if left at that power, so I moved the speed select back to 'ground idle' and switched off the computer completely, which should have caused the engine to run down to this lower speed. Nothing happened!

The only answer now was to fly back to *Atlantic Conveyor* and shut the starboard engine down on finals, using the fuel cock when it became essential to lower the lever to get a descent rate going. Lots of wind over the deck and a willing port engine saved the day, and I landed on without further injury to person or machine.

After landing it was interesting to view the damage. All of the panels in the bottom of the nose door intake had blown downwards from the weight of water that went into the scooped intake, taking all the Dzus fasteners with them. We didn't really have the time or inclination to report all this in the traditional way with an Incident signal, so the maintenance crew just got on with the job of fixing it. They were not far from changing all of the bent or distorted bits when the *Conveyor* was hit by an Argentine *Exocet* missile and abandoned.

Our aircraft went down with the ship.

BIG BOY'S FANSTOP!

Surg Cdr Rick Jolly OBE   3 Cdo Bde RM   1982

In the second half of 1981, the Westland Sea King HC Mk4 Commando variant had finished intensive flying trials and was ready to join the Fleet. The *Wessex 5* pilots of the Jungly world approached this larger aircraft with caution; although delighted to note its greater carrying capacity and higher speed, they wondered about the reliability of an airframe and engine combination that had yet to prove its worth as a replacement for the *Wessex 5*, a helicopter workhorse that had the same sort of reputation as the DC3 *Dakota* of WW2 fame. There were many knowledgeable aircrew around who stated at the time that the best replacement for a *Wessex 5* would be another one - newly minted from the Yeovil production line!

Of course, the *Sea King 4* has now achieved similar status in its own right (as I write this nearly 30 years later), but there were some interesting hiccups in the early conversion process. One very able *Wessex 5* pilot (who later went on to senior rank) found his conversion course slightly truncated by the need to take his new aircraft to war. His experience on the Commando *Sea King* was measurable in just tens of hours when, shortly after the landings in the Falkland Islands, he was tasked to support 3 Para in their operations ashore in the San Carlos area. An emergency call came in about casualties who had been injured in a mortar attack.

The pilot ran out to his aircraft, started it quickly, and with the CO and Operations officer of 3 Para on board, lifted and flew at low level in the direction of the incident. The sharp-eyed CO, standing behind the pilot, suddenly pointed ahead and to one side. The pilot brought the helicopter round in a steep wingover and then, without having to slow down, headed straight for the group that was now visible in the distance. As he came nearer he brought the nose of the aircraft up into a decelerating procedure known as a 'fast stop', where the whirling fan of main rotor blades are brought up to face the airflow, thereby slowing the aircraft.

To fly this manoeuvre accurately and safely, a pilot relies on a mental 'sight picture' to keep his or her aircraft at a secure height throughout, before levelling the fuselage and then maintaining a hover or making a running landing. In this case, his well-learned (*Wessex 5*) sight picture was being utilized in an airframe that was somewhat longer. The tail rotor came into contact with the ground, and the *Sea King 4* landed heavily alongside the wounded Paras.

There were red faces all round as the aircrew stepped down from what was now a big green Portakabin! Another aircraft was found from somewhere, and the casualties were collected shortly afterwards and flown to the field hospital at Ajax Bay They all survived, as did the broken *Sea King 4* (eventually) which became a very useful source of first-line spares during the campaign.

STANLEY POLICE STATION

Lt Pete Manley   845 Sqn   1982

On the way South to the Falklands I was embarked in *Atlantic Conveyor*, and a request came for an armed helicopter to be available for direct airborne support of the assault landings. As I was the squadron's Helicopter Warfare Instructor (HWI) I was expressly tasked to transfer from *Atlantic Conveyor* with a *Wessex 5* 'gunship' to RFA *Stromness* as a solo unit, armed to the teeth. It was fitted with 28 x 2" rockets, a cabin-mounted machine gun and most important of all, two AS12 wire-guided missiles, each with a range of about 7000 yds. Young Ric Fox came with me, and we went ashore as the only *Wessex* gunship, to wreak as much havoc as we possibly could, and based our little unit very conveniently alongside the shore medical facility run by Surgeon Commander Rick Jolly - just in case!

Sadly, no-one asked for the gunship to support them in the right places, or so it seemed to me, but we did have quite an enjoyable time of it preparing to attack other targets of opportunity. Laying down a barrage of 28 two-inch rockets, rippled into an enemy position would have been quite a morale buster, even if we were not able to aim them very accurately - but then the Argentinians didn't know that!

On 8 June 1982, after the logistic landing ships *Sir Galahad* and *Sir Tristram* had been bombed by A-4 *Skyhawks* at Fitzroy, I was asked by Jack Lomas if I thought I could attack a target in Stanley with AS12 missiles – '*Tell me more!*', I heard myself say, eager to see if the missiles worked in anger. Intelligence had established that General Menendez had morning briefings at 0800 in an upstairs room in the Stanley Town Hall, and the powers that be decided it would be a cunning ploy to park a missile on his desk whilst the coffee was brewing, thereby possibly shortening the war. This brilliant piece of 'in your face' aggression had been conceived by Lt Colonel Mike Rose and his SAS team in *Sir Lancelot*.

Jack (our Acting CO) and I flew to *Lancelot* for a fulsome

briefing and whilst we fleshed out the plan, two concerns prevailed, namely anti-aircraft systems around Stanley harbour and the enemy's artillery. It was reckoned that two or three twin-barrelled *Oerlikon* (20/30mm) anti-aircraft cannon systems were somewhere along the foreshore giving protection to the harbour complex, whereas the artillery was scattered, predominantly to the west, but had recently been shelling us during the early mountain battles.

The Oerlikons had a maximum effective range just below my 7000 yds missile range; the artillery, at best guesstimate and even if they were really good, could not acquire and get the first rounds down in less than four minutes. That would give me just enough time to fire 2 AS12s and depart!

To give some understanding of the AS12 *modus operandi*, the launching aircraft has to arrive at a firing position, up to 7000 yds from the target and in a stable hover that is as low as possible commensurate with camouflage, and (of course) in a direct line-of-sight. The target then has to be acquired by the aimer, through a gyro-stabilised sight which is itself joystick driven; the firing mechanism is selected and first missile fired (with a very loud bang and whoosh from the solid fuel propellant) - trailing two thin copper wires through which the aimer's control-joystick commands are sent. This process is one of true 'fly-by-wire' in the strictest sense, and no sticking the crosshairs on the target or 'fire-and-forget' here!

Flares at the rear of the missile aid keeping it visible, positioned just above the target for most of its flight and then dropping down onto the target just before impact. Not as easy as it sounds, because control becomes increasingly difficult with distance (signal time delay) and change in the missile's centre of gravity as the propellant burns gives it an increasing nose-up attitude...

The pilot calls down the time of flight, which is about 30 seconds at maximum range. After impact, the wires are cut and the second missile can then be selected and fired. After the second lot are cut, the aircraft can then vacate the firing position, because at this stage they probably know you are there. Hanging around would be like waving a red rag at an enraged bull!

Practically, a two missile attack should be accomplished in

less than 3 minutes. With all the difficulties and risks seemingly covered and minimised, I thought that the mission could be achieved. As a Helicopter Warfare Instructor I was qualified as a missile aimer, but felt that taking two pilots, one flying and the other as aimer, might be too risky as we could ill afford to lose *two* pilots if things went wrong. I therefore selected Arthur Balls, a fine aimer with much experience (particularly at night and in twilight conditions), and also considered by me to be a better aimer. After discussion he agreed to accompany me and we set about 'tooling up' the *Wessex*.

The aircraft's weapon systems had been checked, but had yet to fire anything 'live' and as this was a fairly risky one-off task, I felt that a practice shoot would benefit us both as well as prove that everything worked. We flew up to Teal Inlet settlement, which at that time was a secure base and also as close as we could get to the front without risk of observation. The practice shot went well, knocking a chunk out of a tiny unnamed island somewhere in Teal Inlet, so we returned to prepare the aircraft and brief an accompanying *Wessex 5* that was to observe from a distance, and come in to effect an immediate rescue if things went wrong and we were shot down.

Early on the 11 June 1982 we set off, flying 'nap of the earth' (*very* low, no rules!), routeing north-east, east and then south to our IP (initial point) below Long Island Ridge. Our planned firing point was approximately 7000 yds north of the Town Hall, in the lee of Mount Lowe, giving us a good backdrop. En-route we made contact with the SAS up in the hills, to establish that nothing was airborne and no enemy activity was likely to disturb our approach.

It was a grey and very misty morning, and I was having real difficulty finding the IP (there was no Satnav in those days, only a map, compass heading and wristwatch), so we kept going until Stanley came out of the gloom and Arthur had a workable view of the target. I reckon that we ended up at around 4000 yds in a very high hover to get the line of sight over Cortley Hill. As all was quiet, we proceeded to engage the target.

Arthur confirmed that he had a good visual lock on the target, selected the first missile and fired. The launch was uneventful, but it lit up the gloom like a beacon and made a seemingly greater racket than usual – nervous tension I suppose. I

74

counted down and Arthur called 'impact'; as far as he could tell it was on target. As nothing had moved and there was no activity ahead of us, we fired the second missile at the secondary target, a *Chinook* parked by Government House that was apparently grounded and our missile was intended to ensure it stayed that way. Just as it left the rail, our comfort zone was rudely interrupted as the world and his dog started shooting all sorts in our direction, though luckily most of it seemed a bit inaccurate.

However, it was undeniably well within range and also traversing towards us, as though searching the gloom to range in on us. Arthur couldn't see what was going on from behind the sight, but for me, keeping still in a hover for 30 seconds was a bit unnerving in the middle of a fireworks display that included some all too visible tracer. At about 20 seconds he called '*lost control*' and then '*fallen short*' and cut the wires. With no more missiles left he stowed the sight and then looked out, to let out a few choice expletives at the illuminations outside which, by this time, were very close!

I dropped the collective, rolled the aircraft right over and with the collective now coming back up under my armpit to full power, we shot out of there like a grouse on the Glorious Twelfth, just as the first artillery rounds started coming down. We made it back to Teal Inlet for a cup of tea (terribly British) and a mental wind down that was made the more pleasant by the realisation that we had got away with it! Eventually the other aircraft pitched up too, having seen the shelling; they had been trying to get close to our position which was obscured by smoke and debris from the artillery. Needless to say they were much relieved to see us back, and both safe and sound - even if a little shaken up!

We heard later that we had missed the Town Hall with the first missile and were somewhat deflated by this, but then cheered by a report from the BBC (and the NY Times on the 12th) that the Argentines were complaining that their hospital ship, '*Bahia Paraiso*' which was alongside in Stanley harbour, had been attacked by a missile from a British aircraft. Our second AS12 had snagged its wires over the ridge and been given the default command to go down and right, taking it into the harbour just short of the ship. This was a pity really - the following night, gunners on the ship opened up on a Special Forces patrol. So much for the Argentine military's *real* feelings about Red Cross neutrality!

Stanley was surrendered on 14 June and I went to inspect the results of our attack. The Town Hall looked in rude health, but the Police Station was not so lucky; its exterior walls were intact, albeit with a small entry hole. However, the interior had been totally trashed – the typical impact picture of an AS12, which was designed with a delayed detonation fuze occurring after piercing the outer shell of a tank.

I spoke to a lady living down the street who went out to investigate the original bang, to be confronted by a cartoon-like scene of bedraggled and smoking Argentines staggering out of the police station! She confirmed that local morale had soared as the story went around.

I then paced out the track of the first missile. It missed the Town Hall by as little as a yard and went down a side street, crossed the main road and burst into the Police Station. It turned out that Brigadier General Menendez did not have a meeting that morning, but perhaps more reasonably, we had not destroyed the Town Hall which was used by our troops as valuable accommodation in the aftermath of the Argentine surrender.

More important than all of that, the Police Station had been occupied by Military Intelligence, and a particularly nasty piece of work by the name of Major Patricio Dowling, who delighted in intimidating the civilian population. He had also behaved in an aggressive manner towards the members of NP8901, the Royal Marines garrison captured when the Islands were invaded. All but one of his subsquent interrogation 'guests' volunteered to return in the Task Force - with the specific interest of 'interviewing' Dowling under their own terms!

We also understood that the attack had given them a real shock, in that we could seemingly pick off a target in the middle of town with such accuracy, with them believing that the police station was the target all along. Dowling certainly got the message and left the Falklands on the very last flight before the British forces secured the airfield.

Although the Marines of NP8901, now members of Juliet Company 42 Cdo RM, were very disappointed not to meet their 'friend' Major Dowling again, it was a pretty good overall result!

NIGHT SBS DROP

845 Sqn   Sub/Lt Paul 'Hector' Heathcote   1982

Early in April 1982, whilst based in Northern Ireland, I'd heard about some Argentine scrap metal merchants who had taken over South Georgia - and thought it would be a wizard wheeze to play an April Fool's joke on my fiancé, Linda. What if we were to be deployed down there to deal with them? I called her and explained that we might be leaving N. Ireland tomorrow - and then sailing to the Falklands, because they were about to be invaded. Linda's earnest response was *"Where are the Falklands - off Scotland?"*

Argentina really *did* invade, of course, catching most of us unawares, including Her Majesty's Government. Not too long after, I was part of the 845 Sqn plan, and celebrated my 21st birthday whilst sailing down the Atlantic to the Falklands. My mother requested the song *'Oldest swinger in town'* to be played on the World Service for me - some accolade!

During passage to Ascension Island in HMS *Intrepid,* most of us were certain that there would be no war and that it would all be over by the time we got there. However, what a surprise it was as we rounded the north coast of the Island - to view the entire and extremely impressive-looking amphibious fleet sitting at anchor. They had been waiting for *Intrepid* to arrive, which was a vital command and control warship. We cross-decked at Ascension to RFA *Tidepool,* an old oiler that had been within 24 hours of being sold when she was turned around from Montevideo and then sailed to Ascension, in order to restore, refuel and pick up a pair of *Wessex 5's* from 845 Squadron.

The journey south included much training in the huge South Atlantic swells - including an unplanned collision at sea with a Type 21 Frigate! We were then briefed that a crew and *Wessex 5* would be required to conduct a Special Forces insert on the night before the British assault and re-invasion, which was planned for the 20th May.

The dream team selected for this evolution was to be Lt Cdr Mike Crabtree, me, and Corporal Kevin Gleeson, an excellent Royal Marines aircrewman (who is now a fully qualified helicopter pilot). Our brief was to transit to HMS *Antrim*, a large guided missile destroyer, then work in conjunction with her own *Wessex* 3 to recce the entrance to Port San Carlos Water - and insert Special Forces as necessary. This was a prerequisite to ensure safe passage for the amphibious fleet's entry in the early hours of D-Day.

Lt Colonel Mike Rose ran the briefing and offered a pint of beer to us all on its conclusion, perhaps as a spot of 'Dutch courage' before we set off. For the recce element of the task, our *Wessex* 5 was fitted out with a door-mounted thermal imaging camera and a very enthusiastic Army Intelligence Corps sergeant to operate it.

At about 6 pm that evening we set off to recce the north coast of the Falkland Islands around Fanning Head. Chris Parry, the Observer in the *Wessex 3,* was to provide radar control for us around the high ground, as we were operating only a few hundred feet above *terra firma*, with no night vision goggles and an insufficient supply of carrots! The recce proved entertaining, as we soon discovered we were being lost in the 'ground clutter' on the *Wessex 3*'s radar. This fact was one we found out the hard way, while moving toward the dark silhouette of some high ground unchecked by our radar controller!

Prudence prevailed and soon the maps came out and we then looked after ourselves, using torches covered in black masking tape (punctured with pin-prick holes) to keep the light to the very lowest level possible. The flight around Fanning Head took us over Port San Carlos, known to be an enemy position, and had us carrying out a swift 180° turn back the way we had come. Around the west side of Fanning Head we heard through the headsets the somewhat disconcerting shrieks of excitement as our army sergeant shared with us the *'excellent news'* that there were lots of enemy down on the ground below, waiting for our Special Forces to come and get them! We flew back to *Antrim* to drop off the Army Int chap and take on board the bare minimum of fuel - and a team of SBS (Special Boat Service) personnel.

Now it was all getting a bit serious; we were briefed to drop the team off as close as we dared to the Argentinean positions, on the reverse side of the hill. Again, *Antrim*'s *Wessex* 3 team were in the area, vectoring us towards the coast - and as a back-up with three 3 SBS chaps on board.

Our first attempted take off from *Antrim* proved disastrous. Maximum torque (rotorhead 'twisting power') on the *Wezzy* 5 was

3200 lbs, with 3500 lbs available for only *two* seconds as a *'get out of jail free card'*. Mike pulled to 3200 lbs and the Wessex became very light on its wheels - but didn't quite get into the hover. In the rolling southern ocean, our unchained helicopter was barely in contact with the ship when a 'kick' upwards from the flight deck brought us to a five foot hover.

Mike was then forced to use maximum power of 3500 to maintain some sort of stability; the situation was unsustainable and our aircraft started drifting down - and backwards. As the *Wessex* slipped backwards off the flight deck, with nowhere to go, it seemed certain that we would crash. Suddenly, the aircraft came to a halt. The designer of the ship had provided us with an unintended restraint, in the form of a rear spotlight housing, mounted about a foot below the edge of the flight deck, and at an angle that created a perfect chock for the tail wheel. This had arrested our rearwards motion purely by chance, but also allowed the main wheels to touch down, so that the boys on deck had enough time to strap us down securely.

What had gone wrong? The brief to the SBS had been quite specific, in that that they must be no heavier than 350 lbs per man. Little did we know that at this point in proceedings, their desire to go into battle heavily 'tooled' with extra weapons and ammunition, had led to a figure of about 450 lbs per man. Their enthusiam had placed the whole operation in jeopardy.

Time was now of the essence and we quickly dropped off two of the SBS to get us down to a sensible weight, for what was this time a successful take-off. We set off again for the Fanning Head dropzone.

Mike and I had come up with a cunning plan, having purloined a single lens night sight from the SBS team. Mike would fly the aircraft and I would describe the terrain and the approach to a 'lights off' landing, half-a-mile to the east of the Argentine position. All was going well until, at about 30 feet on the radar altimeter, not only did my commentary become so inaccurate as to prove useless, we had also lost the benefit of forward air speed and translational lift. With no visual or aural clues to help him, Mike was running out of options. The aircraft entered a series of pilot-induced wobbles, careering across the ground and in no way able to even contemplate a landing. We were forced to fly away at absolutely maximum power, using the artificial horizon and radar altimeter to keep the right way up and away from the ground.

Believe it or not, there really was a Plan B! This involved the accompanying *Wessex 3* positioning for an approach using a 'Doppler hover' over the landing site we had selected. The Doppler equipment detected sideways and fore/aft movement, and then automatically moved the flying controls to correct this and keep the helicopter in a stable hover. Again, all was going well until at some 30 feet, with the radar altimeter-driven height control being 'wound down' to zero for the landing, 'Humphrey' became very unstable. This time, rather than abort, Ian rightly switched on all his lights to sort out the problem - and landed safely.

'Lights' is a small word to describe the lavish display of headlights and hover lights that suddenly turned our night into day, and must surely have alerted the Argentines to our presence. The second part of Plan B was for the troops dropped by the *Wessex 3* to set up a 'T' pattern using their right-angled torches, on which we were well practised at landing. A standard NATO 'T' requires 5 torches but as only three SBS troops had been dropped, we were a bit short on light sources!

The 'T' is able to give you visual cues to advise that you are moving sideways and/or forwards or backwards; also, by their aspect, you can judge your height, although you had to be pretty sharp to get by on such limited information. If you can't actually see the ground, you cannot judge these vital bits of information, and any movement in the inherently unstable helicopter tends to get out of hand *very* quickly indeed.

Our next approach proved much more stable, with the visual cues of the semi 'T' being just sufficient to get us on the ground and drop off our troops. We carried out five further insertions to the 'T' that night. Interestingly, Chis Parry, the *Antrim* Observer, never told us we were all under enemy fire at the time. Thankfully, you don't see tracer bullets coming directly towards you. Anyway, none of them hit, and the work done by the SBS that night made all the risks taken very worthwhile.

After the insertions, we recovered back to *Antrim* for a rest - which lasted only a couple of hours before her 4.5 inch guns opened up for a NGS (Naval Gunfire Support) action onto Fanning Head, at the north end of San Carlos Water. Our cabins were located near the forecastle, making sleep impossible, so we got up early and breakfasted ready to face the day. Walking out onto the upper deck, we were welcomed by a surreal view of beautiful calm waters and a stunning view of Fanning Head under bright blue skies.

We launched shortly afterwards and made our way to the P&O cruise liner *Canberra* for casualty evacuation (casevac) duties. Surgeon Commander Rick Jolly, the Senior MO of the Commando Brigade, was to be our flight medic for the day. He was keen to pinpoit the landing locations of the four units that were now ashore; the first call came in almost immediately, to a fully-laden paratrooper who had slipped off one of the large Falkland tussocks and damaged his back. The man was retrieved quickly, but then a second call came in stating that two Royal Marines *Gazelle* aircraft had lost radio contact and might have crash-landed somewhere past Port San Carlos settlement.

We made best speed in this direction and as we flew over some paratroopers, I asked why they were all walking in line abreast along the ground. A dry response came from our bootneck crewman: *'Because we have probably just passed over the forward edge of the battle area..'*

We were completely unaware that both *Gazelles* had been shot down by a 0.5" machine gun, one into the adjacent Port San Carlos Water and the second onto the ground alongside. We reversed course, executed a few rapid turns while searching and then spotted the badly damaged second *Gazelle*.

We landed close by; Rick Jolly and Kev Gleeson got out and ran over to the crashed helicopter. The two crewmen were dead; it looked as if they had both been killed by machine-gun fire whilst still in the air. We put them in the back of our aircraft to be taken to the *Canberra*, rather than leave them out on the hillside. Rick picked up the GPMG and signal codebooks as well, helped by Kev, who also stated that he had joined the Corps with the dead *Gazelle* aircrewman and had known L/Cpl Giffen well. Such a matter-of-fact comment, as we went back to our business, seemed bizarre and quite astonishing to me.

Back at *Canberra* we handed the bodies, weapon and cypher material over and were then briefed not to bring back any further fatalities, as it was not good for morale! Who the hell were we to pick and choose? No one ever told me that being 21 years old was going to be this difficult...

Around midday, local time, we shut down and got out for lunch and a brief rest. Leaning over the ship's side, admiring the view of the assault fleet and the myriad activities going on was a very impressive sight. An air raid warning 'Red' sounded over the ship's Tannoy system and everyone grabbed a gun and headed for the guardrail. Kev Gleeson had the good sense to unship the GPMG from its mounting on our *Wessex* and then, in a totally Rambo style, started firing at the incoming *Dagger* from his hip - until it passed overhead. From behind us came the warm blast of a *Blowpipe* missile being launched towards the same aircraft as it banked hard and accelerated toward Fanning Head to the north.

The atmosphere became electric as the collective will and expectation of several hundred people on deck followed the missile towards its target. A puff of smoke just short of the enemy jet indicated that the missile had reached its maximum range and self-detonated. One of the Royal Marines muttered about renaming *Blowpipe* as *Slowpipe*...!

Our next task was to go to HMS *Argonaut*, off Fanning Head to pick up casualties from an air attack. As we hovered over the ship's boiling stern wake, we started to winch Rick Jolly down, but were suddenly waved off. An air attack came in and we had to break off, head for land, then alight in a small gully with the left wheel low to give Kevin a better arc of defensive fire out to the starboard side.

As Mike and I sat and watched proceedings, including an impressive line of cannon shells raking the side of HMS *Antrim*, we suddenly realised that we were missing the main event. A sardonic voice in our headsets said: "*Oh, the Doc seems to have jumped out of the aircraft...*" He had done so without warning or explanation! The reason for his rapid exit was soon very apparent as the ground around us erupted, clumps of earth being sent skywards with 'shit and derision' everywhere. As the dust settled, we saw white fibres of metallized 'chaff' floating in the air around us and presumed that the silly buggers in the surface fleet had been firing their seductive chaff rockets in our direction.

However, Kev now advised us that we had been a brief 'opportunity target' for a *Dagger*, which he and Rick Jolly had quite clearly seen heading for us, firing its 20 mm cannons in the process! As Rick was not actually tethered to the aircraft, he had 'popped out' for a moment, before rejoining us from the shallow ditch that he had dived into. HMS *Broadsword* then ripped another Argentine *Dagger* from the sky using her forward *Seawolf* missile battery.

We heard on the radio net that *Ardent* had been badly hit, and spurred on by the sight of HMS *Plymouth*'s *Wasp* racing past below us, carrying our original *Argonaut* casualties back to *Canberra*, we lifted off and sped towards *Fearless* in San Carlos Water. We needed fuel before being able to do anything useful. After refuelling and grabbing a pair of winchable stretchers, we crossed the Sussex Ridge to the west, sighted Falkland Sound again and were immediately aware of the plume of smoke from the stricken ship. In a shallow dive towards her, we got the old *Wessex* up to 145 knots (normal max 120). The stern of the ship was a complete mess of tangled metal and fire, her upper deck full of crew assembling in their bright orange survival suits. HMS *Yarmouth* was bringing her stern alongside to pick up these survivors as they abandoned ship.

Some rapid arm waving then alerted us to two *Ardent*s in the sea off the stricken frigate's port quarter and we quickly moved over to them. Crabbers had been very patient, allowing me to fly all day, but now my inexperience became evident as I struggled to hover over the almost glassy and fuel-slicked sea surface. This provided very few visual cues. Mike took over and the hover became stabilised - so that we were able to rescue the two men, who were both injured and very weak from exposure to the icy water. Because they were unable to do much for themselves, Doc Jolly went down on the wire twice; he physically gripped one in a bear hug and managed to get his winch hook into the life jacket of the second (a rather unothodox technique!) to get them both up into the cabin.

There was little more that we could to help, but Doc Jolly thought the MO might need some assistance, so after we had taken the two casualties back to the medical ship *Canberra*, we then returned to the scene and winched him down. There was no further trade for us that day, and as night fell we proceeded out of San Carlos Water aboard *Canberra*, having spent 13 hours and 40 minutes airborne in the previous 24 hours.

D-DAY - ARDENT RESCUE

Surgeon Cdr Rick Jolly   3 Cdo Bde   1982

In the distance, we could see another attack beginning on the ships at the southern end of Falkland Sound. Having deposited its load to straddle HMS *Plymouth*, a single *Dagger* sped away under full reheat to make good its escape - but as it turned to the west, a thin white line joined it from the foredeck of *HMS Broadsword;* the black dot silently exploded into a tiny ball of flame - then vanished.

We were sitting in XT449, a *Wessex 5* of 848 Sqn, and located in broad daylight on the forward slopes of Fanning Head, witnessing the Battle of Falkland Sound - and waiting for another air attack. It was quite an unpleasant and powerless feeling. Corporal Kevin Gleeson RM, the aircrewman, pointed past my shoulder as four more Argentine *Daggers* began an attack on HMS *Antrim*. The fourth aircraft turned away from this attack, heading directly toward us with the leading edges of his wings twinkling with cannon flashes. Cpl Gleeson immediately and defiantly started returning the fire. I dived out of the helicopter into the nearest ditch, expecting the *Wessex* to be obliterated, but seconds later when I lifted my head the Wessex was still there - and the *Dagger* gone. My departure was noted coolly by pilot Mike Crabtree's comment: *"Oh, you back with us then, Doc?"*

Out on the thin grey line of warships, although some distance away, we could clearly see a column of smoke rising from HMS *Ardent*, backed up by an urgent message on the tactical radio, giving her four letter callsign. We discussed the situation. Should we go and assist, or wait until all signs of attack had gone? It was our decision as no-one else was available to ask. The inspirational answer came in the form of Lt Cdr John Dransfield in HMS *Plymouth's* little *Wasp*, streaking past below us with the casualties from *Argonaut*, heading for *Canberra*. We lifted off and made best speed towards *Fearless* as our fuel was perilously low. As Mike Crabtree and his co-pilot Hector Heathcote refuelled, I jumped out and grabbed a couple of winchable stretchers.

We took the direct route across to *Ardent*, over the Sussex Ridge, flying as low as possible in the belief that this was all enemy held territory. Downwind of the burning ship, an acrid smell pervaded the air as we flew through a thick pall of black smoke. The *Wessex* came to a hover just off the port quarter and about 30 feet above the slick-covered swell. What a sight! The Type 21 frigate lay still in the water, listing and drifting. Her lovely, classic lines had been obscenely defaced by some demented giant who had smashed in her helicopter hangar and opened up the flight deck edge with an enormous tin opener. Deep inside this enormous blackened hole, the fires of Hell were burning, with a bright orange intensity that was overwhelming. *Ardent's* survivors were grouped mostly on the upper deck forward of the bridge, some already in bright orange survival suits, but almost all were pointing into the sea off the port quarter.

The pilots then spotted two survivors in the water and immediately moved the *Wessex* into position above them for a rescue. Whilst this was going on, the elderly frigate HMS *Yarmouth* was being expertly positioned by her CO, Commander Tony Morton, stern on to *Ardent's* bow. Survivors were scrambling across from ship to ship. However, it was obvious something was wrong with our intended rescue, so I moved over, on all fours, to the door.

Looking down, I could see instantly what was wrong. The man in the water was drowning and quite unable to help himself into the rescue belt. The strop was dancing around in the rotor downwash and the chap just didn't have the strength to grasp it. I knew that something *had* to be done fairly swiftly, and I also realised that it was down to *me* to do it...

I had been given some winching experience and training back at Culdrose and was still smarting from my chicken-like behaviour at Fanning Head, so I indicated to Kevin Gleeson that I was ready to go down on the wire and attempt a rescue. I could see him talking to the two crew up front, probably expressing his doubts that I would be able to make any useful contribution!

Command approval was given, quite literally. Mike Crabtree knew of my Fleet Air Arm background; I was soon in the strop, going down to the water. A lot of memories came back to me at the rush - winchmen usually had a proper immersion suit and a winch hook with a braided copper wire extension in order to earth the aircraft to the sea before this happened through the 'winch weight' (*me!*).

There was no time for niceties here though; the really unpleasant electrostatic shock through my body just preceded the even worse physical shock of immersion. Later on, I was told that the water was 3 degrees Centigrade, but all I knew at the time was that a numbing cold instantly enveloped my whole being as I gasped for breath. I could also feel my heart rate slowing and my peripheral vision blurring.

All the while, Mike Crabtree, with some marvellous precision flying, was towing me across the swell toward the first man. The desperate look on the chap's face, his wild thrashings and punctured life jacket said it all. A fresh adrenaline surge kicked in and I forgot my own discomfort as our outstretched hands touched and then gripped. I spun him around in the water and gripped him in a fierce bearhug, my fingers locked together in front of his chest. There was no other way of lifting him...

Mike very gently lifted the helicopter about ten feet and Kevin then slowly winched us up from the sea. My left shoulder had been wrenched and hurt like hell, but I knew that if I let go, our survivor would slip back into the sea - and we'd never see him again.

The aircrewman then displayed genuine skill and strength in getting us both into the cabin, using very small winch control movements with his left hand whilst gripping my clothing as I came up to the door. With great strength, he hauled us both into the cabin, where I collapsed on the cabin floor - we'd done it! I compressed the casualty's chest hard, looking for some confirmation of life, and was rewarded with a vomited gout of sea water. The young lad then opened his eyes and was violently sick again. I breathed a huge sigh of pride and relief and sat on the canvas troop seating, realising that I had done at least one *really* useful thing in my life...

Kev then looked across the cabin at me, with a questioning frown on his face. I gave him a thumbs up, but he now indicated that there was another man in the water beneath us - and that I had to go down *again,* to get him! Seconds later, I was back in the strop and being lowered to the sea surface once more.   I had no idea what I was going to do when I reached the survivor, but knew that my wrenched shoulder would not hold out against the load this time.

As I spun on the winch wire, I saw a mad *Cinerama* projection - first, *Ardent* burning, with her crew watching from the deck, then *Yarmouth* backed onto her bow, followed by *Broadsword* (which had moved in close to give anti-aircraft cover), then Grantham Sound - and *Ardent* again.

Then I saw a new sight on the merry-go-round.

Lying there quietly in the swell, arms outstretched and blood streaming downsea from amputated fingers on his hand and a huge cut on his scalp, the second survivor watched me with uncomprehending eyes. He later told me that he could not see the winch wire that I was suspended from and actually thought I was the Archangel Gabriel coming to collect him!

BANG! The horrible static electricity discharged through my body again, but quickly passed - and I was now in the water alongside him. I knew I was now too exhausted to lift him manually, but as luck would have it, his life jacket had lifting beckets on it. As the winch wire went slack at the top of a swell, I managed to hook him on to the winch hook that my strop was attached to. Instinct had kicked in just at the right moment. It shouldn't really have worked, but it did - and we were soon back up in the cabin, where Mike ordered the door to be shut and heaters placed full on. Feeling soon returned and we delivered our precious cargo to the *Canberra*.

Postscript: In Canberra they'd been very busy and as dusk fell, the surgeons were able to swing into top gear. A quick tour of the 'Club Bonito' revealed our two rescued survivors, both asleep but comfortable. Both had injuries of sufficient severity to require morphine. I noticed that one, the young Able Seaman, was lying next to an Argentine casualty that we had lifted earlier in the day from Fanning Head! It was also very important to us that both these gallant Ardents, Charge Chief Ken Enticknap QGM, and Able Seaman John Dillon GM, survived - to receive their subsequent decorations for gallantry, in person, from Her Majesty The Queen.

MY FIRST MERCEDES

Lt Pete Manley   **845 Sqn**   **1982**

Shortly after the fall of Stanley there was a dearth of wheeled vehicles, particularly at Port San Carlos. We had (naturally enough) come ashore with none at all, but now that things had quietened down a bit as far as hostilities were concerned, we needed to be mobile occasionally. I had spotted an Argentinian *Mercedes G-Wagen* up a nearby hill, both partially hidden by a dry-stone wall and camouflaged quite effectively. Moving quickly, I managed to get two bomb disposal Royal Engineers to come and check the vehicle for booby traps before trying to lift it out. This was a rather important administrative move, because there had been some reports of booby-trapping by the departing invasion troops!

On getting back to the site, I found that a *Sea King HC4* had just landed close to the vehicle. I asked the pilot what he was up to, as this vehicle had already been allocated to 845 Sqn – well, at least it *sounded* official! He said 'finders keepers' and stated that it now belonged to 846... Wrong answer! I then asked him if he had checked for booby traps? This question was followed by a long pause, at which point I said that I had some Army experts who were about to do just that on behalf of 845. Another long pause - and after a few choice words over the ether, the *Sea King* shuffled away – good result!

After checking that no grenades were attached to the vehicle, we started to prepare for the lift, clearing cam nets and getting rid of some rocks that were in the way. My man on the ground *did* notice that the whole loom of ignition wires had been casually hacked apart, so we couldn't move the vehicle by starting it and driving. Well, not until the 'Greenies' had fixed that loom anyway. I had been told by my crewman that they weighed around 2000 lbs, but being a prudent type had allowed a little extra for comfort; I also knew that crewmen are prone to exaggeration, so I reduced the fuel load to allow about the same as for an FFR Landrover (about 3100 lbs).   After a little messing about, we attached the strops and began to attempt a lift which, despite full power, had absolutely no result.

Wow! This is heavy, I'm thinking, maybe we ought to get it light and try to move it on its wheels? This seemed a good plan, so I landed beside it and got the aircrewman to jump out and make sure the handbrake was off and that it had a clear run down the slight slope in front of us. Just one minor snag - the vehicle had a dry stone wall, which actually looked pretty feeble, right in front of it and also in the direction of the slight downhill slope.

OK, so the next plan is to rock it back and forth a bit to knock the stone wall down. My helicopter is now 12 feet above the *G wagen*, hooked on with a strop - and I have a gleam in my eye. I rock it forwards and backwards, against the 'feeble' wall, quite unafraid that I might scratch the paintwork. Good Heavens! This is war and it won't affect my no claims bonus... Once the wall was mostly down I could drag it over the rubble and down a smooth slope. Easy. It worked just as I had carefully planned, but I didn't reckon on the truck taking on a life of its own and rumbling off down slope with me and my helicopter in tow, both trying hard to keep a grip on the situation!

I could feel the aeroplane being dragged bodily along and must say I didn't like it very much. In fact, I was about 'pickle it off' (release the lifting strop) when I got help from that good old pilot's friend, Translational Lift. This aerodynamic phenomenon cuts in at about 15 knots of airspeed through the rotor disc and gives a huge lift bonus, requiring substantially less power to achieve the same airspeed. That means there is substantially *more* power available to provide lift for your load, including your recently delivered new *Mercedes*!

It came unstuck and we flew very gingerly all the way to the 845 Squadron drop-off point; I knew in my heart of hearts that this was a *very* big load, because it hung vertically down without any movement. Realising that I was going to be unable to hover, I approached in a very gentle, slightly flaring descent. The *G-wagen* was fortunately facing forwards (loads on a strop do tend to spin slowly) as its wheels kissed the ground and I pressed the cargo release switch to 'pickle' it.

Before anyone else could bag it, I landed alongside to put my mark on my prize and also inspected the *Mercedes* for damage. There was nothing too serious - apart from a few dents and of course the ignition wiring problem. On checking the door pillar ID plate shortly after that, I could hardly help but notice that the weight stated was a little higher than I had been led to believe, at 2600 - not in pounds but in ruddy *kilos*!

This little number weighed in at around 5720 lbs and my maximum lift was firmly pegged at 3100 lbs - over a ton too much. We checked the aircraft very carefully, but there were no signs of overstress, which just goes to show how strong the *Wessex 5* was.

FOOD LIBERATION

Pete Manley, again!   **845 Sqn**   **1982**

We had fought the war, which was mercifully a lot shorter than had been predicted when we embarked upon it, and suffered the many unpleasantnesses associated with living in the field or makeshift barn type accommodation. We had been supplied with food by the ships and RFAs of the Task Force, but they could only carry a limited amount of course, so we had to 'make do' as far as the catering was concerned. The locals did what they could for us, but we were a huge force compared with the tiny island population. We were not in any way starving, but did manage the odd dream or two about a nice juicy steak surrounded by crinkle-cut chips with mushrooms on the side.

One of the first edicts out after the cessation of any hostilities is '*No Looting*' and this war was no exception.

However, shoreside, just below and along from Government House in Stanley, there were a load of shipping containers full of goodies that needed 'checking'. This was at a time when fresh provisions (particularly meat) were hard to come by out in the field, or 'camp', from the Spanish word '*campo*', and any opportunity to procure was welcomed. I happened to be making a visit to Stanley and landed beside said containers to shut down and await my passengers. As a result, I had time to do some of that 'checking'.

Inside them was a huge stock of Argentinian rations which had never got to their front line. In amongst this treasure trove was a pallet full of 2.5 kg tins of beef stew – a fantastic prize and after merely a moments salivation, I wound into action. The crewman and I carried, lifted, shifted, heaved and grunted - all the time looking surreptitiously over our shoulders to ensure we weren't being bubbled. We soon managed to get the whole pallet in the back. Quite fortuitously we were waiting to transport a senior officer, one Ewen Southby-Tailyour Royal Marines, to the racecourse and beyond, so we soon had some impressive 'top cover'!

Ewen was something of a living legend, having spent some time in the Islands prior to the Conflict; being a 'yachty', he had hand drawn coastal charts which were subsequently copied and used in the invasion. He was happy with our little plan and not in the least bit concerned with the slightly doubtful origin of our goodies. The racecourse had been used by Argentinian C-130s for stores drops and was littered with debris and once-only parachutes, fairly flimsy devices of thin fabric but of an incredibly tough cross-weave.

I picked my approach line to avoid as much rubbish as I could and came on in, but just as we flared for touchdown I could see a torn section of parachute lift up - and begin its seemingly magnetic and inevitable flight towards us. Swiftly shutting the engines down and trying to get the rotor brake on was to no avail. The large segment of parachute caught on a blade and then passed across the tail section which decelerated the blade so quickly it tore out the drag damper. The second blade - also now free of constraint - took its own route through this new gap and clipped the cockpit just above my head before diving into the ground, keenly followed by the final two who had lost the will to survive on their own.

Throughout the event I managed to keep the *Wessex* upright, but we had spun through 180º and now faced a bemused bunch of Paras who then proceeded to clap, whistle and generally applaud the spectacular arrival of one now unserviceable helicopter. Having clambered out of the back, Ewen began saying something witty about 'a good landing was one that you are able to walk away from', when he saw the wreck. Being the gentleman he was, he also decided the Paras should stand guard over the wreckage and its contraband contents until a more serviceable aircraft could be brought in.

The crewman and I spent the waiting time clearing

anything looking vaguely like a parachute away from the landing area alongside my wreck. Having managed to procure another Squadron aircraft fairly quickly - with the promise of stew that night - we loaded this one up hastily and completed the task. You may think all that effort for tinned beef a bit strange, but believe me, on that night the stew tasted like the finest fillet steak!

The broken aircraft remained where it was in the stadium for a while, but then got lifted out in pieces under a *Sea King* and was ultimately rebuilt to fly again back in the UK. No injury was sustained by any personnel, apart from bruises on my inner thighs, but believe me I was extremely wary for any signs of FOD after that.

Ewen never lets me forget this episode whenever we meet, on the grounds that this was the only time he's ever crashed whilst babysitting!

SEA KING SOLO

Surgeon Cdr Rick Jolly OBE   Falkland Islands   1982
(Note by JB: Rick is a doctor and a total Fleet Air Arm enthusiast, but has never been formally trained as a pilot - or held any type of flying licence, military or civil!)

The war had ended, it was a sunny day and we were going home that evening in *Canberra*. I was keen to say thank you to the Junglies for their fantastic support throughout the campaign; they had brought the great majority of our casualties to us, and then moved them out to the Hospital Ship *Uganda*. I rode across to Navy Point and said my piece to them, several times. 846 Squadron immediately offered me a ride in one of their *Sea King 4s*. The Ops officer knew that in reality, I was a complete plane spotter and would seize this opportunity gladly – which I did! I should also explain that through some generous friends, I had clocked up a few disjointed and definitely poor continuity hours in various helicopters, not least during a previous tour of duty at Culdrose, the home of Royal Navy helicopter training...

The mission this day was to fly back to the area around San Carlos and pick up as many as possible of the *Rapier* anti-aircraft missile firing units that were still positioned up in the hills surrounding the anchorage. The pilot was an old acquaintance, and with only an aircrewman in the back to assist him, pronounced himself glad of my company. Very soon, I was flying the easy sectors in between the more difficult load-lifting phases, during which the *Rapier* units could behave a bit skittishly beneath the helicopter on a long strop - and needed a steady and more experienced hand.

The weather was wonderful, the visibility fantastic and I was completely relaxed and happy. The instructors back at Culdrose had taught me well in the jaunts I had enjoyed there in the *Gazelle* and soon I was doing the take-offs and landings as well.

We refuelled in Stanley at one stage and then flew west once more. The pilot then indicated that he would like a 'comfort stop', and the crewman chipped in that he needed one too. No problem for me - I asked for the pre-landing checks, completed them and then brought the aircraft round in a gentle descending turn into wind before settling on the soft tussock grass. The pilot grinned at me, gave me a 'thumbs up' signal, unplugged the intercom, undid his harness and climbed out of his seat – to disappear down the back.

All the engine instruments indicated operation within normal limits, but a quick check outside revealed that I had landed just below the crest of a slight slope. As a result, I could no longer see the horizon to the west. That was the direction from which a threat might materialize and an attacking Argentine jet on some kind of last-ditch raid could have arrived right on top of us without any warning. The solution to this problem seemed obvious, so I lifted the *Sea King* back up into the hover, moved forward steadily using the cyclic trim button - and put the aircraft back down on the grass again, about sixty yards away.

The junction between sky, land and sea now stretched right across all the front cockpit windows. I sat there and waited, 'fat, dumb and happy' as they say in aviation, until I heard the pilot re-enter the aircraft through the main cabin door. He almost ran up towards the cockpit, and looked a bit flustered as he strapped in rapidly.

I asked him: "*Everything OK?*"

"*Well, yes – Doc – everything is OK **now**...*" he replied, followed by: *"Why did you move the aircraft?"*

As I began to explain, it suddenly hit me. Without the consent of the aircraft captain I had done something seriously illegal, flying one of Her Majesty's aircraft without permission as well, not having done the approved course and so on. It was time for some grovelling apologies to counter my thoughtless action.

We then took off in silence, but after reassuring himself that I hadn't bent anything, the pilot suddenly grinned and handed control of the aircraft back to me. He thought a bit more, then announced: *"If you want your log book signed, Doc, then the minimum time of flight that I can approve is five minutes and not twenty-something seconds..."*

He paused again:

"Congratulations on your first solo, sir - and the beers tonight are most definitely on you..."

JUNGLIES IN THE MODERN ERA

DURACELL

Lt Andy Jeffrey   **846 Sqn**   **1983**

Whilst in charge of a small detachment ashore at RAF Akrotiri, Cyprus, undertaking the modification of aircraft for the BRITFORLEB support in the Lebanon, I overheard the maintenance crew talking in hushed tones about something that they had planned for that evening. Always being someone up for a good run ashore I listened intently to see whether this was going to be one worth gate-crashing. It didn't sound too good - as there did not seem to be any mention of booze, loose women or even food. However, I soon realised that this had the potential to land me in deeper water than the pluckiest run ashore of all time.

The hangar next to the one we were using was home to an American 'sneaky' squadron operating the *Lockheed U-2* spyplane. As ever, these aircraft were heavily guarded by both the CIA and Navy *SEAL*s but the Yank Special Forces team had now got used to our lads' presence just next door - and they did not regard the

Brits as any sort of threat. The unit had two aircraft, one operational and one fully stripped, undergoing deep maintenance.

The *U-2* is modular in construction and with wings, tail plane and forward pointy bit all removed, the fuselage was no more than a black cylinder. The engine was out and the fuselage was wheeled in and out of the hangar every day to create space for the hangar to be used for maintenance operations on the other bits.

Our imaginative bunch of maintainers had acquired a pot of gold paint and some brushes, then made some very professional looking stencils; they were about to give the black cylinder a new identity with a gold band around one end and *'DURACELL'* along its length. Despite my protestations that they would be shot - or certainly incarcerated for many years - if they were found by the *SEAL*s anywhere near the hangar during the night, my observations were just laughed at! The smallest of *SEAL*s made a member of the Prince of Wales Company of the Welsh Guards look like a toddler! I just *knew* for sure that as Detachment Commander, I would be ending my days in Sing Sing or somewhere similar...

The lads had already been into the hangar on a number of occasions to measure up the intended recipient of their artwork. Fortunately, their resolve was such that I was able to bribe them away from their intended night out by taking them all out to dinner, which may have cost me a fortune in the short term - but at least it allowed me to complete my Naval career and draw the pension!

TRANSIT TO SAILLAGOUSE

Lt Andy Jeffrey   **846 Sqn**   **1983**

We were a six aircraft formation in loose vic, en route from base at Yeovilton to the Pyrenees for a week of mountain flying - and all looking forward very much to it. We had had a fairly dodgy meteorological scene painted for us but the boss, Black Mac, was keen for us to get on with it. Approaching Bordeaux above a layer of cloud, we had not seen the ground since crossing the Channel. The boss chatted to us on the squadron private frequency, briefing us to carry out individual instrument recoveries to Bordeaux, our fuel stop. This was not too easy, because we had to do radar approaches, 'talked down' by the controllers and often the French accents weren't easy to understand. Much easier by far to do it visually if we could.

Coffee, sandwiches, newspapers etc adorned the cockpit for the transit - I had the honour of having a wonderful man, the late Bill Sample in the left hand seat as captain of the aircraft. Suddenly a hole in the cloud appeared and resulted in our leader entering a death-defying spiral descent followed by numbers two and three, but without a word of warning on the radio! Poor old Bill had to decide whether to cap his flask, drink his coffee, abandon his sandwiches or clutch Linda Lusardi tightly to his breast as we, number four, followed the rest into a rapidly dwindling hole.

Through 'egg and cress', or more likely curry sandwiches in Bill's case, I vaguely heard something akin to 'head north so we don't hit the blighters', by which time I was well over half way back to the Channel with the same thought in mind! It did seem a long way down, most of which was in cloud, all the while aware that there were three aircraft ahead, which I could not see, and a further two behind that I could also not see, the hole having disappeared completely by now! No real surprise when we popped out underneath the cloud at a bit under five hundred feet above the ground to find that we were now on the *tail* of number six a couple of hundred yards ahead, who had 'followed' us through the same hole behind number five! Phew!!

A few days later, when a squadron *'banyan'* (picnic) to the beach was planned, our junior rates were faced with a huge decision - go for the ball or for boobs? Whilst they were innocently enjoying a splash about in the sea with a football, a bus load of squeaky-voiced, lumpy-fronted honeys from the local finishing school parked at the top of the beach. The doors opened and the beach became littered with uniforms and underwear as the girls shed their clothes and headed for the water where they tried out their English on the poor young sailors. They struggled hard to avoid practising their Braille technique - not completely successfully.

There was a considerable amount of loud squeaking in French, with the occasional phrase of pigeon English thrown in. With that as a backdrop, our esteemed boss was 'holding court' with his officers a little way along the beach when another extremely attractive young thing set up on the beach right in front of them.

She proceeded to remove all clothing bar her skimpy bikini bottom, in a positively seductive garment-by-garment manner - no haste, just pure erotic suggestion, whilst casually ignoring her goggle eyed audience. Bless him, the Boss could barely contain himself and gave his audience a fairly detailed and loud account of what he was willing to do, if she asked him nicely as each item was removed, fully assuming she couldn't understand a word he was saying. By the time she had given herself a good layer of 'cooking oil' to aid the tan, it was touch and go whether or not his heart would be up to much more work that afternoon.

She then reached into her bag and pulled out a banana, which she peeled with the same seductive style that she had undressed in, almost reducing our man to tears as he told his boys graphically what he could offer as an alternative. As she slowly moved the banana toward her lips, she changed her mind at the very last minute and extended her arm towards the Boss and asked him, in a very strong North country accent:

"*D'ya wanna bite luv?*"!

THE UNICYCLE TEAM

Lt Mike Abbey   **845 Sqn**   **1984**

In 1984, during the final years of the *Wessex 5*'s operational service, I was the Qualified Helicopter Instructor (QHI) of the premier jungly squadron (or so we thought). My CO at the time was Colin DeMowbray, who was very aware that 845 were losing the tactical advantage to 846 with their new shiny new *Sea King Mk4*'s. Ever alert to his surroundings and the underlying ethos of the moment with in this case, a stroke of genius, DeMowbes, (as he was always known) saw an opportunity to wrestle the initiative back from our sister squadron by forming a unicycle team.

So, the unicycles were purchased, aptitude tests conducted and six pilots, all too slow getting out of the crewroom I suspect, were selected for the honour of representing 845 on the unicycles!

Much practise was enforced on the unlucky half-dozen - up and down the corridor and then out on the squadron dispersal, hard effort which all paid off eventually as bruised knees began to be a thing of the past. He slowly brought the team up to a standard that would have made Coco the Clown proud. Having mastered 'straight and level' the bold CO got them formation cycling, including formation changes like the **Dead Sparrows**, all complete with oxygen mask-distorted cries of "*Swan, swan,.... NOWWW!*" and so on. The fame (or should that be 'notoriety'?) of the team spread like wildfire, of course, eventually getting to the media via some kind of defence leak - well they happen all the time, don't they?

The media link did pay dividends with an invitation to attend the TV show *Game for a Laugh*. The only problem in the way of this bold move was a 3 Commando Brigade exercise due to take place in Northern Scotland at the same time. The exercise involved transporting Royal Marines from HMS *Invincible* to shore and then on numerous troop moves around Scotland, culminating in a massive battle against some unfortunate troops who wore 'Jockfrocks' in their spare time! The *Wessex* had been sidelined during the majority of the exercise in favour of the *Sea King*, due to our comparatively limited lift capability and *its* superior speed, so we were simply going through the motions by putting out messages every now and then to let people know we were still there. Little did we appreciate that, towards the end of the exercise when the shiny new *Sea Kings* started to go un-serviceable, the good old *Wessex 5* would be called on to perform.

Imagine the scene then, a lonely QHI (me, because I had been sharp enough to get out of the crewroom before the unicycle team was selected), sitting in the Command Post (CP) on top of a mountain in Scotland in the middle of the night. Sitting was possibly a poor description, as after five days of being ignored by everybody I may just have dozed off in my sleeping bag, while lying down on my thoughtfully provided campbed!

It seems I hadn't actually heard the many radio calls that may have been made from HQ over the preceding couple of hours to start getting *Wessex* airborne; I was awoken from a deep sleep by the approach of a *Gazelle* landing outside! Imagine my surprise when the Brigade Commander burst into my nice cosy tent and kindly helped me out of my camp bed by tipping it up with his boot.

"Where's your bloody CO?", he snarled, certainly not a very happy chappie and was definitely not in the mood for a nice fireside chat. *"I'll go and get the Senior Pilot, Brigadier - sir"*, I responded. I'd learnt at an early age to blame senior officers for everything, but it didn't work this time.

"I don't want to see your bloody Senior Pilot..", he shouted even louder than before, *"**where** is your tosspot of a CO?"*.

When staring at a Very Senior Bootie whose face is turning the colour of claret, there is only one thing to do - run! He hadn't bargained for this and although he lunged towards me, he was too late to stop my scampering out of the back of the tent and legging it away into the night. I returned sheepishly, at least ten minutes later, with the Senior Pilot, Les Port, who had also been sleeping and needed to waste time by dressing etc. Ten minutes was probably about eleven minutes too long, as the Brigadier was considerably more agitated now than when I had left him.

Les spent a fruitless few minutes trying to chat about the tactical situation, tell the Brigadier some of his awful jokes, deflecting the many questions relating to the Commanding Officer's parentage, before realising that the only thing he could do was come clean: *"Well Brigadier - it's like this, the CO has taken the Squadron Unicycle formation team down to RAF Abingdon, Oxfordshire to take part in an ITV programme with six of our aircraft. Very sadly, the other two seem to be unserviceable, but we are working on them as fast as we can..."*

We watched the Brigadier go through the preliminaries to some ritual war dance, while the colour of his face changed from bright red to white as he expressed his feelings verbally, loudly and may I say very lucidly, asking in the process why **six** aircraft had been needed for this task.

"Well sir -" replied the Senior Pilot, *" - the six aircraft fly in formation over the Unicycle team whilst they are formation unicycling, and it just wouldn't be the same with only **one** helicopter..."*

The Brigadier then rose to his full height of what seemed like 7' 6"; despite our concerns, he did not then have a heart attack. Instead, he quietly walked out of the CP, climbed into his *Gazelle* and disappeared.

"I think that went quite well - considering..." I said to the Senior Pilot in a vain attempt to make what had been the sinking of the *Titanic* appear to be merely the chinking of ice cubes in a glass of gin and tonic. 'Splot' looked at me in that classic Senior Pilot manner which makes you realise that *you alone* have just ruined his entire career! I have to say I felt wretched for several minutes before the reality kicked in and I watched him, shoulders bent and head down, walking slowly towards the nearest payphone to try and alert his leader to the load of unpleasantness that was about to descend on him from an enormous height!

WHITEOUT

Lt Cdr John Beattie   *Clockwork* **cell**   **1984**

In 1969 the Commando Squadrons started carrying out annual winter warfare training at the Royal Norwegian Air Force (RNoAF) base, Bardufoss, 167 miles inside the Arctic Circle; this was part of the commitment to defend NATO's Northern Flank and known as Exercise *Clockwork*. The first detachment, by 845 Squadron, was hastily organised whilst the squadron was on the way home from the Far East. They just didn't stop at England!

On arrival in Norway they found all their kit wholly inadequate, as no provision had been made for specialist cold weather equipment whatsoever. However, things did improve in terms of knowledge, equipment, training and facilities over the next three decades. Alongside the RNoAF and Army, I believe that the Royal Marine/Commando Sqn combination became the most proficient of NATO's operators in the region. During my own time there we were constantly liaising with the American forces - and invariably giving them advice on *'how to do it'*!

I was the Senior Naval Officer Bardufoss (SNOB) between 1983 and 1986, when we ran three courses per winter, each of one month duration. The first week was devoted to lectures and practical tutorials, which involved living in the field, usually grouped as single aircraft units known as 'Eagle' bases; each consisted of a pilot, aircrewman and a maintenance team of seven ratings. Ski-ing and snow-shoeing were essential elements of this phase, because you are often unable to move at all in soft fresh snow without being able to do one or the other. Living in tents at -30 deg C also takes a little getting used to; lessons about the differences between camping and surviving in temperate and arctic climates are many and varied.

In addition, the aircrew also spent a further couple of nights 'escaping and evading', which (of course) involved living out in the wild without the tent! In this case the escapees made ample use of the silver birch trees which grow like weeds in Norway, to make *'bashas'* for protection and warmth. The second and third weeks were then spent operating the aircraft from a cold airfield dispersal rather than the warmth of a Norwegian hangar, as well as carrying out any required maintenance or repairs, even engine and gearbox changes using improvised shelters.

Many good lessons were learned here, as flesh sticks to metal at temperatures of -15 deg C or below, and the maintenance staff had to be constantly aware of this fact in the field. We Flying Instructors taught the students to carry out snow landings, fly safely in the mountains, load lift and how to navigate over featureless terrain by day or night - and so on. Snow landings are a vital skill; on many days soft snow is the surface of choice, which of course billows into a cloud when subjected to rotor downwash. This removes all vision outside the immediate vicinity of the aircraft, whereas normally you would use the natural horizon and middle distance objects to assess aircraft movement.

During a snow landing you have to find an object which stands out against the snow - a tree, an exposed rock or perhaps a bergan (rucksack) that you have thrown out of the back of the aircraft during a low pass. This you now focus on during the latter stages of approach and land right alongside, ignoring all else.

The final week of the course is spent at war with the fiendish *Red* forces. The detachment takes to the field, initially in a flat, easily accessed site where communication and movement between elements is not a problem. Once the team are used to field telephone and radio communications, means of re-supply and so on, the enemy attack, usually at 0200, severely testing the impromptu defences run by a group of Naval air mechanics! It's all good fun, with many rounds of blank ammunition expended and the sky lit up with *Schermuly* flares.

This signals a move to less amenable facilities, up a mountain and with some distance between the Eagle bases making the business of communications and re-supply a real-time problem - and potentially quite difficult! Helicopter tasking in support of the friendly troops carries on unabated, but now domestics begin to matter, particularly as the weather can be unpredictable and Eagle bases are easily cut off from outside sources.

During one such move, a young *Wessex 5* pilot, both an excellent chap and very good aviator, had carried out an early morning troop move and then come back to collect his Eagle base team and their belongings. On this first sortie, he had some trouble with the aircraft's Auto Stabilisation Equipment (ASE) and felt he should do a little investigative work to help the maintenance team in pinning down the problem.

The ASE has a panel fitted to the rear centre console, which is over the pilot's left shoulder; it houses a set of 'lane isolation' switches, combined with a meter to tell you what each 'lane' (of control input/output) was doing. Simple diagnostics could be done by checking each lane individually on the meter to see if all were getting a signal and then perhaps isolating any you chose. The snag was, it was over your shoulder and not easy to see or operate while trying to fly at the same time.

On this particular morning there was of course no sun, as it wasn't due to appear above the horizon for a month; the weather was grey and overcast, with moderate to poor visibility. Our pilot had bundled his team and their bergans into the back of his *Wessex* and was flying down a valley into a large bowl-shaped area, surrounded by snow-covered mountains, into a very white, featureless and flat landing site. He raised the helicopter's nose slightly to reduce speed, and then looked back over his shoulder to select ASE lanes on the meter. When he looked forward again, he became totally and hopelessly disorientated.

The inner ear contains semi-circular canals which are lined with minute hairs waving around in a thick fluid. As the head moves, the fluid flows past the hairs and they register movement with the brain. So, inside your brain you *know* that you are moving, but the eyes have a very strong veto over this process and visual cues will generally blot out this 'apparent' movement if it didn't exist in the first place. In this case our pilot turned his head fairly smartly, thus moving the fluid and giving him the impression that the aircraft was turning; but the view outside the window did nothing to change that perception. All he could see in any direction was a white curtain, as though a piece of plain white paper was being held around and in front of his eyes.

At only 500 feet or so above the surface, it wasn't long before the aircraft was going downwards in a spiral descent. It impacted the ground at a 20 degree dive angle, doing around 90 knots, ripping the rotor system and main gearbox off the transmission platform - and depositing them about 200 feet ahead of the wreck in the snow. The pilot was quite badly injured, having sustained a chest injury, and lost quite a bit of blood. The chap in the left-hand seat was bruised, but still strapped into his seat, despite it being now separated from the aeroplane and 100 feet away from the wreck!

The men in the back had all been thrown to the front, mostly because despite regulations and 'rigorous' training, none had strapped in! The aircrewman, Pete Imrie, had been on his dispatcher's harness and took quite a fierce hit from the door frame. He ended up hanging from his middle by the harness belt.

Luckily, the area was close to Setermoen, a military camp, and help came very quickly. Paramedics on the scene decided that the pilot and aircrewman had injuries serious enough to warrant immediate air transport to the major hospital at Tromso, some 65 miles to the north. One of the other *Wessex 5s* picked them up and started off, but the weather was deteriorating quickly and *en route* became abysmal. He ended up having to land in a snow field close to Bardufoss. Within a couple of minutes, a Norwegian Air Force UH 1-B *Huey* beat its way in from over the horizon and transferred the patients.

This *Huey* also had some considerable trouble making its way towards Tromso, but had the advantage of a pilot with an intimate knowledge of the local area. He did fly over 5 miles of the route following the amber flashing light of a snow plough, just 10 feet above the road! There is little doubt that he saved the life of our pilot, who made a complete recovery and returned to spend a distinguished career in the Royal Navy before joining the airlines, and the aircrewman also lived to tell the tale, became an officer and had a most rewarding career. All in the back enjoyed their celebrity status for a few days!

Back at Bardufoss, we celebrated after all seemed to be OK again - by hosting a party for the UH-1B squadron, feting our gallant and brave *Huey* pilot, eating the junk out of reindeer hooves, and beating the Noggie aviators at all the mess games we could think of!

DIAL-A-MAP

Taken from an Article in *Cockpit* Magazine   Timeless!

The Squadron CO decided he would personally carry out the task of a VIP lift for an Army General, then take him to his Headquarters with the assistance of the Squadron Chief Aircrewman. These were the days before satellite GPS (Global Positioning System), when our only navigation equipment was a map, compass, watch - and sufficient training and practice to get pretty much anywhere in the world using initiative, intuition and invention!

The brief was simple; fly to a grid reference, remain rotors running and then telephone a number to advise the General - who would come out to the helicopter immediately. It was a lovely day, and our crew enjoyed the trip in quite stunning weather, agreeing with each other that England really was a beautiful place to call home. They found the grid reference with no trouble at all, deep in Army country - and verified by the Chief's many and various navigational checks on the run in, just to be absolutely sure, because you can't afford to make a mistake with the squadron CO up front!

The site turned out (predictably) to be a military barracks, which seemed very reasonable, but there was a parade in full swing there, with neat lines of soldiers, all with rifles and fitted bayonets on their shoulders, plus the Regimental goat looking resplendent in his dark blue and gold coat showing the regimental crest and battle honours. It all made sense that they had the right place. The CO landed a little way apart from the actual parade, though still on the parade ground, mindful of his proximity to the troops. Obviously, the General had been taking the salute or some such arrangement.

However, not much happened for quite a while and six tons of Westland noise-generator throbbing away proved a little too much for the parade adjutant, who approached the helicopter making the well known military signals for *'Get out of here NOW!'* The Chief Aircrewman at this stage clambered out of the back, indicated that he needed to make an urgent telephone call - and was duly led to a nearby building. Meanwhile a group of fairly angry-looking senior officers gathered near the helicopter, to be waved at occasionally by the pilot, all the while wearing a huge grin.

Soon the Chief returned, and quickly jumped into the back, uttering the immortal lines: *"Sir, I think we'd better scarper, and fast. It seems that we've gone and landed at the phone number - while I've been trying to ring the grid reference!"*

CROQUET

Lt Andy Jeffrey   **846 Sqn**   **1984**

My Squadron, 846, was in Norway and I had just come back from the Gulf supporting the minesweeping effort for the *Armilla* Patrol. We had one aircraft left at Yeovilton; after a good deal of arranging various permissions, I flew to my home town of Aberdyfi in West Wales with a couple of new pilots, two aircrewmen and about eight maintainers. The plan was to satisfy the long standing promise of an exercise with the local RNLI Atlantic 21 rescue craft, have a night in my local pub - and then an exercise with the mountain rescue team the following day.

During an excellent night in the pub I was accosted by an old friend who many years earlier had started an annual croquet match between the local Outward Bound staff and the village. He was the Outward Bound's guru in respect of the 'Queensberry rules of croquet' and was mortified when, after a run of around four years of unchallenged victory, I was recruited into the village team and the tide turned. Having been taught by a Royal Marine and coached by the Royal Navy, thus negating any form of 'official' rulings, they didn't really stand a chance!

Despite ongoing accusations from the Outward Bound team

of 'cheating' (how can you cheat at croquet?) the village put up a string of victories by always ensuring that I was around for the annual match. The argument in the pub that particular night became somewhat heated and ended in a challenge to a 'straight' match the next day. Sadly, I discovered that neither of the two sprog pilots or the aircrewmen knew the game, but not being one to give up, I gave my old chum 'Splunk' a call at around 2100 to see if he could turn up the next day at around lunchtime. He argued a very good navigation training case with his Squadron first thing in the morning - and the game was on.

However, in the morning, the challengee informed me that he would not be available as he was now building a log cabin in the forest for Outward Bound use and would not be able to get to Aberdyfi at the appointed time. There were many good reasons why the transit time was just too great. *"Not a problem"* said I, *"just give me the grid reference and I will sort it out for you.."* Poor Splunk had a little fancy footwork to do getting official permission sorted out, but at the pre-arranged time, the chap was beside himself when a 'paraffin budgie' duly came to the hover above a hole in the trees at the grid reference he'd given and lowered a winch wire and strop to whisk him away. He alighted on time and the game was duly played, loosely to the Queensberry rules.

Luckily the ploy worked and their team succumbed to yet another crashing defeat. On that sunny day, two Royal Navy *Commando SK4*s were neatly parked on the only piece of flat ground within easy reach of mountain rescue and RNLI assets, but one which the 'Light Blue' refused to use because it was too small!

PRESSONITIS #2

Cockpit **Magazine**   **1985**

The Squadron CO was leading an 8-ship formation from his base at Yeovilton north to Arbroath, the intention being a 'visual rules' (VMC) flight with refuelling stops at Shawbury and Carlisle. Met predictions for the day gave warm sector conditions running the length of the UK with low stratus and hill fog warnings in force. It was not a wonderful forecast for the intended trip; bear in mind that in those days the *Wessex* 5 carried no navigational aids, and flying in cloud was only undertaken as a last resort! The problems of flying in cloud lay not so much in doing it, but getting back to earth after you'd had enough of it. The *Wessex* had no on-board means of getting down, with the military preferring ground based radar approaches (GCA). This gets you to within 200 feet of touchdown and in the right place, but civilian aircraft preferred the on-board Instrument Landing System (ILS). It had therefore become the norm to '*Grub Navy*', when faced with poor weather away from the sanctity of military airfields, to carry on at low level under the cloud. This was OK until the cloud comes down and meets the ground!

Add to this a military penchant for using only UHF radios and the civilians VHF, you had two groups unable to talk to each other. Someone realised this serious mistake and a few VHF sets crept into service as bolt-ons, but most squadrons in the '70s and '80s only had a couple of sets each. This flight had only one such set, in the No 4 aircraft...

The flight up the Bristol Channel went well with a cloud base of about 1000 ft, but three miles west of Chepstow the problems started, with the cloud base lowering and the higher ground ahead disappearing in hill fog. The formation was now in close line astern and the search was on for a clear northerly valley to get through to the lower ground toward Monmouth and Hereford. At last one valley looked promising enough, the leader reducing his speed and descending to very low level. The inevitable happened, of course, and as the valley narrowed, the cloud lowered, so leader flared to slow down - as did each aircraft behind him. This was the forerunner of the modern motorway 'concertina' effect; by the time it got back to No. 8 he had to break away and climb up into cloud, there being nowhere else to go.

The remaining seven executed a 'valley turn' in formation and departed south back to the Bristol Channel, to try and find No 8. He, meanwhile, having done a little cloud flying, let down gingerly into a clear area near the Severn Bridge and eventually rejoined the flock. Leader then decided, with the formation complete once more, to continue up the Severn Valley via Worcester and Telford at a far healthier height and thence into Shawbury for a now much-needed refuel. The weather 'actuals' from Liverpool and Warton indicated bad weather both inland and northward, so a sea track up to Carlisle via the Dee estuary became the planned option. The departure from Shawbury was uneventful except for the worsening weather that was visible out towards the Chester area. Leader then chose to clear Hawarden to the west, unfortunately towards the higher ground, to be met by low stratus and hill fog. Back they all went into close line astern, down to *very* low again and about 35 kts airspeed and proceeded up the A55 on the correct side of the road!

Now the problem lay in the National Grid system, the pylon tops of which were in cloud. This was solved by eight short excursions into cloud and over the pylon tops, but with two sets of these to clear, it proved to be a rather interesting and nerve-racking experience! Shortly after this the cloud lifted sufficiently to see the Dee estuary a few miles to the right; after a 'dirty dart' at low level, the formation was happy again, some five miles off the coast with visibility at 5 to 6 miles. The long flight around the Lake District and into Carlisle was uneventful, except to check the paintwork of a few fishing boats.

A coffee break was then taken at Carlisle to calm the nerves and top up with max fuel for the long final haul up to Arbroath. Little did the aircrew know that much worse was to come! The plan from Carlisle was to cut across to the Newcastle area, hopefully into better weather, then proceed up the east coast to Arbroath. The low stratus was still evident on take off from Carlisle and 700 feet above ground level was all that could be managed - but with clearer weather to come, or so the Met man had said.

Twenty minutes later it all happened again; Leader had been gradually descending and slowing in worsening conditions when suddenly he and the remainder of the formation hit a vertical sheet of cloud. The first seven took standard cloud entry actions, breaking onto pre-determined headings and climbing as fast as they could, each now unable to see the others. Number 8 was more fortunate in that he just managed to keep clear of the cloud but overtorqued (pulled too much power) in the process. He did a swift 180 degree turn and diverted back to Carlisle, but was not forgotten.

Meanwhile, the seven remaining aircraft had successfully

completed their 'blind' bomb burst but (unbeknown to them) were now in the let down lane to runway 07 at Newcastle Woolsington, with a BAC *1-11* passenger jet being marshalled in their direction for its final approach on the Instrument Landing Sysem! The radar controller at Woolsington probably had an impending coronary when he saw seven radar echoes passing the outer marker, going outwards like the ripple from a stone being thrown into a calm pond!

The No 4 at this stage began apologising profusely over the only serviceable VHF radio set in the formation, trying his best to explain the situation, whilst being badgered by his CO on the UHF radio, demanding to know what was going on! (You can listen to both radios, but of course only transmit on one). Needless to say, he couldn't actually tell the controller where the others were, or at what height they were, or when they might stop climbing...

The BAC *1-11* full of passengers was sent off to orbit the pattern and landed after the helo 'formation' had eventually cleared the area. The Leader broke cloud first, at 3500 ft - with the remaining six breaking through in quick succession shortly after, but now spread up to 15 miles apart from their Leader and sandwiched between two heavy stratus layers. The *Wessex* has a UHF homing device called a *Violet Picture Homer*, a simple needle that points left or right towards a transmitting UHF radio on the same frequency. Turn your aircraft until the needle is in the middle - and you must be heading towards the transmitter (or directly away from it). After a bit of homing, the formation had managed to join up again and a course was set for Arbroath in visual conditions, on top of cloud at 4000 ft.

A rough position was obtained from Newcastle Radar by No 4, in the knowledge that there was no further radar coverage until RAF Leuchars, about 80 nautcal miless to the NNW. Fifty minutes later, radio contact was made on UHF with Leuchars Radar and homing for a radar-controlled let down requested. A slight tremor of panic then spread through the formation when Leuchars replied that their radar was on maintenance, as indeed most radars tend to be when you need them most!

Leader, now left with little alternative, elected to home to the Leuchars overhead by UDF, then execute individual let-downs out to sea through some 3000 feet of cloud. Leuchars Met gave 2 miles visibility with a cloud base of 1000 feet, but this was lowering rapidly with a 90% probability of fog in the very near future. Leader called the formation to hold above cloud, then descend individually; down he went and three minutes later called VMC at 900 feet and cleared No 2 to come down. This process continued for the next 15 minutes, with each aircraft breaking cloud 100 feet lower than the one before, culminating in No 7 obtaining visual contact with the sea at 300 feet on his radar altimeter.

The now dispersed group continued 10 miles up the coast toward Arbroath, encountering scattered sea fog in increasing quantity. The first five aircraft managed to get into Arbroath in visibility not exceeding 300 yards, a challenging task at the best of times. Nos 6 and 7 were less fortunate and hit much thicker fog, resulting in their unscheduled landing and shutdown for the night on an Army range six miles to the south.

For the first seven aircraft, the day was over, which with the fuel states they were now at was fortunate, but for No 8 at Carlisle, the excitement was all to come. After diverting back there, the pilot phoned Yeovilton to report the situation and stated that he would stay put for the night and try the next day. However, in the best tradition of 'press on regardless', he was persuaded by a senior officer to depart immediately and try to at least get through to Leuchars that night. Leuchars were still giving reasonable Met conditions when the pilot checked with the Carlisle Met chappie, but the remainder of the formation knew otherwise. However, when they phoned back to Carlisle to advise No 8 of the actual situation, they found out that he had just departed!

Leuchars were informed by phone without delay and told to divert No 8 into Edinburgh Turnhouse as quickly as possible. He did call Edinburgh for radar control on his UHF, but as radio communications were found to be unworkable on the common UHF frequency, the pilot decided to change to the emergency frequency for further assistance. This worked well and he eventually carried out a successful radar approach into Edinburgh, breaking cloud at about 500 feet. In doing so, that pilot successfully carried out his first ever diversion on a still shiny and new 'White card' - the beginner's instrument rating.

Ten hours after the first take off, all eight aircraft were safely down, albeit in three separate places and with not too much fuel left between them. On the following day the skies cleared and the formation rejoined at Arbroath to start the less risky business of emplaning and deplaning troop drills, plus load lifting. The crews also acquired some time to reflect on and repair their shattered sense of security and also to regret their twin-engine complacency…

TREVOR 'Lead Boots' JACKSON

Lt Mark Evans RM   **707 Sqn**   **1987**

It was sometime in 1987, when 707 Squadron were living in the Nissen huts overlooking X-ray Dispersal Site behind the control tower at Yeovilton. John Beattie (BT) was in charge of perhaps the most outrageous, outspoken and out-of-their-depth bunch of Jungly beefers there had ever been - and it was great fun indeed! For reasons connected with not enough serviceable aeroplanes and too many students the Sea Harrier training squadron had got into the nasty habit of launching at 0800 every morning. 707 Sqn had therefore been volunteered to provide the necessary SAR cover for the inevitable PAN or MAYDAY that accompanied Harrier flying.

It just so happened that a lot of hard-standing re-surfacing was being undertaken at various locations on the airfield at this time; one of these tasks included parts of X-ray Dispersal. As a formally 'contracted' evolution, the whole process of re-surfacing was not happening in a hurry; the various areas under re-construction were cordoned off and out of commission for weeks at a time whilst the concrete was first laid - and then allowed to cure. The 'out of use' areas would be briefed every morning at Shareholders, which happened at 0830 hrs on 707 Squadron.

It must have been a big week-end at home, because Anna was at work early and Trevor was doing his famous 'one-armed paperhanger' impression, feeding their girls, doing the washing up, shaving, eating his wheaties, sweeping the floor and - on this special morning, scorching his only uniform white shirt with the iron. Not one to be put off by such a minor event, Trevor went straight to the dhobi basket and pulled out last week's flying suit, then gave himself a bollocking for not getting the dhobi done over the week-end, then slipped into the somewhat crumpled *Grow-bag* before setting off to work.

Being a Monday morning, we must have all been keen to get the week going, hence by 0755 most of the team were sitting around drinking coffee and telling lies about how much they had made on Norman's latest 'shares scam', when in pops our Senior Pilot Mike Crabtree: *"Hello boys, who's covering SAR for the stovies? Well, that will be you Trevor I suppose, you're certainly dressed for the part. Did you sleep in that flying suit or what?"*

The contractors had been hard at work all week-end, digging out the old concrete. By 0810, they had just put the finishing touches to the newly laid top coat of a big area in X-ray Dispersal. This, of course, had involved the delivery of several truck loads of ReadyMix and to allow the trucks to get close to their drop points, the crowd barrier cordon had been removed.

At 0800 came the pipe: *"Do you hear there, this is Air Traffic Control, good morning, the airfield is now open, stand-by for the Crash Alarm and Tannoy Alert Check..."* The stovies launched, but about 15 minutes later the clangers went off noisily again, followed by an urgent sounding pipe: *"Sea Harrier XYZ with fumes in the cockpit is 10 miles east of the field and has declared an emergency. Emergency services close up at the base of the tower, scramble the SAR helicopter..."*

Trevor reacts like a startled gazelle. He's on his feet, eyes big and wide, fully focussed, helmet in hand and racing down the corridor for the northern exit, not saluting his Commanding Officer as he shoulders him out of the way and more importantly, not acknowledging the very well-endowed young Wren blocking his path - most unusual - hey, this chap is *really* concentrating! A sharp right turn this side of the Ladies' toilets, a couple of strides across the grass and he's onto the dispersal area, heading for his mighty steed, which is parked just about as far away as is possible on the far side of the tower...

It's now about 15 seconds after the Tannoy call and every man and his dog (707, 845, ATC et al) have taken up good goofing positions overlooking the airfield - because you don't want to miss a good crash - and if you actually saw it happen, then you can't be on the Board Of Inquiry! When Trevor hits the edge of the newly laid, very recently smoothed and *very* wet concrete, such is his speed and natural grace that his first three paces leave no evidence of his having even got up that morning! The fourth breaks the meniscus, by the fifth he's ankle deep, and the sixth up to his shins with boots and leg pockets beginning to fill.

He can now hear the laughter coming at him from all directions - even the navvies who were leaning back on their shovels admiring what was, until a few seconds before, a magnificent job. Trev has by this time almost come to a standstill, with the fluidity of his graceful progress slowly but surely diminished a little more with each step, as if in a Walt Disney cartoon...

'This is just like running through wet concrete -' he thinks to himself, *'- hang on a minute, this IS wet concrete!*

The 707 duty aircrewman, running abeam Trevor but on dry land, has caught up with and is now overtaking him, but is having problems seeing because of the tears pouring out of his eyes. The duty driver and Medic from the Sick Bay are driving erratically due to belly-laughing and almost all of 707 and the complete complement of the tower are by now incapacitated as they witness Trevor in his finest hour - well, it certainly seems like an hour to Trevor!

Eventually, and I mean *eventually*, he made it to the aircraft with concrete up to his knees, helmet covered in the stuff and at least one glove lost in the fresh mix. Just about everyone inside the airfield boundary was crying with laughter. Trevor was fuming so much that he could not see properly, but nonetheless somehow managed to get the aircraft started and made the call..."*Sea King Zulu Charlie, ready...*"

He was just in time to hear "***Sea Harrier XYZ has landed safely, emergency services stand down - and nice one Trevor!***"

When Trevor was appointed away from 707, his friends were good enough to present him with a fully serviceable flying boot duly mounted in its own concrete plinth. To this day, it is still used as a door stop at Trevor and Anna's home in Keinton Mandeville, and he only charges a bottle of red for a look at his 'concrete foot' should you be interested!

ODE TO THE WESSEX

Lt Cdr David Baston   CHOSC   1988
(Reprinted from *Cockpit*)

Well, it's gorn, - finally and irretrievably *gorn*. A lovely old helicopter that was already an elderly design when Westlands (those well known makers of garage doors) got their hands on it and turned a single piston-engined, American design into the twin turbine *Wessex 5*. The stories surrounding the aircraft are legion and its reputation for rugged and safe, if not always reliable flying, made it a firm favourite with those of us who were lucky enough to fly it. I suspect that never again will we have a helicopter that has such a superb single-engine performance and such enormous reserves of power when both were running. Some of the torque figures pulled are firmly burned into the minds of those who just kept pulling on the collective lever to avoid impending doom!

There was a well known Commander (Air) of a Naval Air Station who managed the ultimate in Australia by pulling so much torque that the complete rotor head came off. He must surely hold the record for over-torqueing, though I am sure that as a Helicopter Warfare Instructor (HWI) he wouldn't admit to *ever* looking at the torque meter, even if he'd known where it was. Luckily the head came off on take-off, so the dozens of Australians occupying the fourteen available seats came tumbling out of the back, whingeing but unscathed.

Engine-off landings were a fertile area for experiment and it surely was one of the few helicopters that could be safely 'engined off' without having to use the collective lever. All it took was bags of nerve, even more speed than normal and a certainty that no one important was watching you! The trick was to utilise the flare, quite precisely, to reduce ground speed and rate of descent to arrive with little of both, then roll the tail wheel on early and - the brave and clever bit - tilt the rotor disc rearward as the front end lowered itself to the tarmac. Minor problems were always in the back of the pilot's mind, such as too much rearward tilt and you chopped your own tail off! This made it a spectator sport of some note, with many cries of "*Chicken!*" over the radio to the not so brave, as it was very obvious when someone cheated and used the lever at the last moment! Did I say *cheat* by using the lever?

Strength at all ends of the machine was always a great bonus. No one who saw the brilliant arrival in dispersal, after an air display rehearsal at Yeovilton, will forget one Squadron Commanding Officer's dashing arrival as he bounced the tailwheel off the top of a ground power unit with a good twenty degrees nose up, recovered, then landed for the second time in front of his surprised and by now rather nervous marshaller. There were also the chaps in Singapore who returned to dispersal after an Instrument Training trip (supposedly being conducted at several thousand feet) that had a goodly portion of the main telephone cables between Singapore and Kuala Lumpur wrapped neatly round the aircraft's nose and undercarriage! It was bad luck, that one, because they only hit them while avoiding a train...

A particularly good demonstration of the ruggedness of the old girl was also amply displayed on an Instrument Flying (IF) trip in Cornwall. The pilot under test was the Squadron CO, who had the added disability of being a Royal Marine to whom IF and quite a lot of other things (like holding a knife and fork) did not come naturally. Well, at the end of the trip the aforesaid RM was actually on centreline and glidepath, so the IRI (Instrument Rating Instructor) decided to let the *Jolly Green Giant* continue below break-off height under the hood to see what happened!

Well, the *JGG* just sat and held everything nice and steady, locked onto the instruments, with the result that the aircraft struck the ground a shrewd blow at a steady 90 knots, sticking there as if superglued as the combined team of IRI and RM *JGG* could not work out what to do next - or even who had control at that stage! 'Wings' knew what to do though; he picked up his phone with one hand and watched the aircraft with binos in the other, because if you see the disaster you legally cannot be on the Board of Inquiry! Well, the aircraft passed the tower slowing only slightly with faint wisps of brake dust beginning to show, and a fairly impressive amount of rearward cyclic finally caused the aircraft to come to a halt halfway down the rather long runway. The subsequent debrief was not entirely dominated by the IRI, as is usual, but Wings certainly had an awful lot to say.

To my certain knowledge it is also the only helicopter ever to have successfully taken on a *Sea Harrier* in air-to-air combat and won, forcing the damaged 'stovie' to return to base unable to continue his sortie, whilst the victorious and gallant *Wessex 5* crew, of which I was the Captain, landed in the car park at a nearby inn and celebrated their historic victory.

This followed a mid-air collision in cloud and resulted in a little cosmetic surgery being required around the tail wheel area of the *Wessex* plus a new tailfin for the *SHAR*. Spookily, the Air Traffic Team on watch at the time happened to be husband and wife, one of whom was controlling me and the other Willie MacAtee, a US Marine Corps exchange pilot in the *Sea Harrier*. More importantly than these key details was the fact that husband and wife had 'withdrawn ambassadors' at the time of the incident - and subsequently divorced!

If the *Wessex 5* had a weakness, it was its tendency not to start when it was really necessary. It damned well knew when you were on a VIP trip and would flatly refuse to start, but then after the chap had departed, fuming and late by car, it would start as though nothing had happened! The attitude of 'Command' was always to have a spare for a spare for a spare, especially at long weekends, to ensure the job could be done. The dodgy starting was made worse in later years by the air engineers changing the batteries to smaller ones without telling us operators. This certainly made going home for lunch, or stopping off at a café or beauty spot whilst in transit, a much more exciting business!

No one to my knowledge ever got caught out by the powers that be, but several *Wessex* have been known to fly quite long distances, on *one* engine, to places where it could then be admitted that the other would not start! It knew when things were really serious though and rarely failed on a SAR mission, or on one glorious occasion in the days of short exhaust pipes, when an aircraft in the middle of a line of 18 others on Salisbury Plain did a wet start and set fire to the grass. The others all started wonderfully that day, thank goodness, and rapidly flew away from the now-raging fire!

When it first went out to Borneo this tendency not to start, especially when hot, meant that you did not shut down whilst pausing between tasks. However, to reduce fuel consumption and noise it was common to pull the speed selects back to about 200 rotor RPM or less (they would normally be at 230). The interesting bit came when you took off, especially if you forgot to push them back up again. The aircraft would stagger into the air (and if you were lucky down a slope), its rotor blades coning like a ballerina's arms whilst you struggled to get the revs back - without the passengers knowing anything was amiss and, of course, before you struck the trees!

Radios were another interesting quirk of the early *Wessex 5*. It had a marvellous HF set that could receive every known commercial radio station from all round the world, plus the ability to talk clearly to Malta from the Culdrose local area. What it could not do, however, was to talk to Culdrose from the local area or any other Naval Air Station from any other area! Whether this was due to the Ops Wrens spending more time on their nails (or perhaps the Ops Chief) than listening to deafening static for hours on end, we shall never know.

To go with this marvel of technology, the *Wessex 5* was fitted with a truly remarkable UHF radio, the PTR 170. This was a lightweight set designed for the *Whirlwind* with the fantastic total of 12 crystallized channels and nothing else. The *Whirlwind* was lucky as the set was not ready in time, but instead of ditching it, some communicator who clearly had a vested interest in the thing (probably future employment with the manufacturer, though anyone who would support the PTR 170 would make a doubtful employee!), kept the project alive and then bolted it into the *Wessex 5*, presumably thinking that's where it would do least harm. Even though 12 channels may have been adequate in the '60's and '70's, they were understandably always the wrong 12 channels.

Now you may think that Junglies have always enjoyed spending their lives flying as low as possible, but this is not so. We would have loved to join the 'pingers' flogging around in the clouds, idly glancing at instruments that patently lacked the correct attitudes, but *we* couldn't talk to anyone. The only answer was to keep as low as possible and talk to no-one. After all, if you are lower than a delivery van, which does not have to get permission to enter the Heathrow Control Zone, why should *you* bother?

I had better clear up the low flying business, as the *Wessex 5* spent most of its life there. To fly as low as possible is clearly still a prudent course of action, never mind the lack of radios that forced us down in the past. If anything drastic should go wrong, you are

117

much closer to that which is going to break your fall. Just ask anyone who has fallen off a barn roof (as indeed I have) and he will tell you that 'height hurts'. Teaching students to fly the *Wessex 5* was another interesting pastime, as anyone who has followed the saga of modifications to the fuel computers and the plethora of Pilot's Notes to go with them, will testify. Luckily, once again the fantastic single-engine performance made up for any lack of speed in dealing with these things, while giving the instructor time to look up the correct actions as the student struggled with the wrong ones!

The total lack of drama when on one engine was well demonstrated by an experienced Pongo on an exchange posting. On his final handling check at the end of his conversion course he did autorotations, approaches, landings and take-offs, all without noticing that the port engine had not been advanced from 'ground idle', where it was no good to man or beast. On his re-scrub he did little better, so was returned to the Army where his single-engined flying skills were more appropriate for their single-engined aircraft.

The airframe did not always escape unscathed from these training exercises. Witness the two instructors who were practising EOLs (Engine Off Landings) by pulling the Speed Select levers (throttles) back on each other in increasingly difficult places. One pulled them at 100 feet on climb out; the other chap realised things were beyond salvage and invited the perpetrator to sort things out! He was unable to intervene and failed to do anything positive, so the rotor RPM decayed drastically and they crashed straight ahead. The crew then had to climb out through the back of the cabin, as there was a main wheel gently rotating outside one pilot's window and the ground filling the other!

The *Wessex 5* has certainly seen life all round the world and its starring role in operations and disasters like the 1977 Fastnet Race during its history are well known. Its greatest asset was that it was *fun* to fly. You may not have been able to see much out of it; you may, even now, have a bad back from its appalling seats; you may well never have seen your crewman's face while in flight, but it was *fun*. You could chuck it about all you liked and just as long as you were smooth with your green-gloved mitts, it would do almost anything. Only retreating blade stall, tail rotor stall or your seat collapsing as the adjustor sprang out from the vibration, would let you know that its limits were being approached!

Will the *Sea King 4*, with its readily-cracked airframe ever engender the same affection? With more radios than Currys, a 'defensive' suite that tells you you're being shot at, plus the bootnecks in the back able to see if you have got the right map, I doubt it. What about thirty degrees angle of bank the maximum, and vibration that would shake the spots off a raddled tart? Pah! Fancy not being able to land with over forty degrees nose up for fear of breaking something! The Commando assault at Air Days will never be the same again! Imagine, unlike the *Wessex 5*, not being able to fire rockets at your unarmed enemies (naturally we would never dare use them against someone who can fight back!)

No, we won't see the likes of her again, and more's the pity, but the venerable, lovable *Wessex 5* was certainly amazing FUN while it lasted...

MILK RUN?

Lt Andy Jeffrey   **846**   **1989**

We were at sea in a mixed ship, with junglies and 'pingers' co-located, always a very volatile situation and the basis for a considerable amount of 'sport'. Winding up the pingers by getting all the Helicopter Delivery Service (HDS) 'jollies' allocated to us junglies was a technique that ranked high on the list. This was normally a quiet afternoon's flutter around the fleet, calling at various ships on the list with mail and stores, dropping off or picking up personnel.

On this day I was tasked to go to USS *Very Big Carrier* in my *Sea King 4*, drop two American passengers, pick up eight, or maybe eleven passengers at slot time 1725, and then return to Mum (my own ship); it would be a piece of cake. Bearing 340 - Range 120 miles, but might be 153 miles; two contacts in the vicinity, but no problem, I'll take stacks of fuel, go north for about an hour then use the UHF DF (Direction Finder) - should locate him nicely. The aircrewman is damned good at his Dead Reckoning navigation, and Mum's nav updates and PIMs are usually pretty accurate. Pleasant banter on telebrief during start up - really friendly team on this RN ship, a pleasure to work with, shouldn't really be a Carrier Vertical Strike (CVS), would be much better employed as a Landing Platform Helicopter (LPH). CVS of course normally carries *Sea Harriers* and anti-submarine helicopters, whereas a LPH carries the real thing - Junglies!

Start No 1 engine, spread the blades, programme the TANS nav computer, get the Automatic Flight Control System (AFCS) checks out of the way - plenty of time in hand. Start No 2, engage rotors, but notice an unusual, slight flickering of the 'Blades Spread' and 'Flight Position' lights with rotors turning - looks like a glitch with the slip rings, so no problem, but I will warn the maintainers that we may have difficulty getting it folded on our return. Rest of the checks good, get nav update - OK, Air Ops reckon that USS *Very Big* is now tracking south, no great surprise as she was heading about 160 degrees at 15 knots when we were there about two hours ago, so 'off lashings', 'out telebrief' and lift - smack on time!

Long transit past the Amphibious Group - good recognition stuff, routine 'ops normal' calls, a milk run really, but very boring - and the pingers call these 'jollies'! *'Hello Very Big this is me where the hell are you?'* We should be able to see them from here, 'cos 1000 feet up you can see for ever, and USS *VB* is as big as a small town; vis is excellent apart from one shower falling out of that rather large cunim cloud over to the east. Try another call and use the D/F this time: *'Hello Very Big this is me...'* – and we get an answer, but the D/F kit cuts down the reception quality; must be some distance off, never mind - at least we have a steer, albeit straight towards that rain shower...

Get her visual, call their Flyco, oops sorry, I suppose you are big enough to call yourself 'Tower'. I can hear our *Sea King AEW* asking on the radio if he can get off their deck. If he gets away before us, he will probably open towards Mum at slow speed and wait for us - they're not bad guys really, even if they are pingers. Oh - do we have enough fuel to join on their starboard quarter and hold? Yes, but if you could get me on for just a couple of minutes I will get out of your hair straight away...I see, a fixed-wing recovery inbound - only take twenty minutes, no big deal, plenty of fuel. OK, and we enjoy watching until they are all down, so if we slow up a bit we might get onto their deck from this lap of the holding pattern.

USS *Very Big* then declares that we'll have to wait another thirty minutes. Hey that wasn't in the brochure, but still plenty of fuel, no big problem, stovies (jet pilots) are the same on our ships too, not very flexible, as well as demanding first of everything. Hang on a minute, how long have we been airborne since the Senior Maintenance Rating said three hours clear before maintenance is due? Go to TANS Data 9 - very expensive clock this, but never fails, been airborne one hour forty-five minutes! USS *Very Big* is now heading 110, but Mum is heading 160, so opening out - and we understand that she is going to increase speed in the next couple of hours. Bit of a developing situation there, hairs on the back of the neck starting to tingle. Took an hour and twenty minutes to get here, but if *Very Big* had been in the right place we would have saved ten minutes. Mum is now almost due south at around a hundred and fifty miles, so if we leave now we will be back on board within the three hours.

'Hello Very Big any chance of squeezing us on quickly?' Not just yet I'm afraid is the resolute answer, but it was worth a try as I am starting to get fed up with my position in the starboard hold. Nice sunset though; they could have used this image as a sequence on the set of the film *Top Gun*. Punchy stuff, these American carriers.

OK it is now dark, we have watched a recovery, a launch, another recovery, a second launch and an unscheduled recovery of a stovie with nav kit problems; we have thirty minutes to Minimum Landing Allowance, and over two hours in the Starboard Delta hold under our belts so far - how about letting us on deck? Finally, they call us in on their version of a radar controlled recovery. Maintaining 060 as instructed, crossing the stern, bit of a long outbound leg, radio is awfully quiet, switch to other aerial, is it my radio or theirs? Select 'Guard' (emergency frequency), ah there you are – *make your own way in and clear to land*. It seems that call signs and radio frequencies changed five minutes ago, and of course I didn't expect to be anywhere other than in the bar at this time, I was not carrying new call signs - and had forgotten all about the possible frequency changes. Oh dear!

No idea where Mother will be now. A night transit to Mum is probably going to be over an hour and a half with eleven passengers using DR nav, plus a dodgy UHF D/F for homing at the other end; unsure what the next maintenance item is, but confident I am able to go through the usual 10% extension, as well as going through some very impressive-looking electric storms to the south of us - I think I will shut down and plan this one carefully, rather than just refueling and heading south...

USS *Very Big* says I'll have to fold if I shut down and then be pulled out of the way. They have lots of planned deck activity coming up. So, into 'accessory drive' we go, but the normal lights are flashing and winking along with a couple that should *not* be there. Rats! What a time for the blade fold system to decide to wrap its hand in! Better see if any of the RN guys we are picking up know anything about the system - after all, they have an AEO (Air Engineering Officer) with them, so we should be in safe hands...

Wait - just who is this idiot shouting at me? I can do without *his* input - I've got a helo that won't fold its blades, blocking a runway the size of Heathrow, an Air Boss who is giving hostile vibes over a radio that has now decided to work again (I hate it!), a Flight Deck Officer who looks as if he might pick the aircraft up bodily and throw it over the side if I don't obey his definitely '*non English speaking*' gesticulations, and undoubtedly a whole sky full of stovies who are keen to come home for their milk shakes in the next few minutes - and this idiot seems to want to know why I am shutting down! Oh, now I understand - oh, it's the aforementioned Brit AEO.

OK *Shag* (the co-pilot) you stay there, I'll climb out and see what the hell we can arrange in the way of folding this beast. Outside, plugged into long mic/tel lead, I'm amazed at how many people can actually get up the side of Mr Westland's dark green climbing frame. Someone up there knows about the manual blade fold valve; the main rotor blades move at last and now resemble a very expensive version of a Venetian blind, but with one of the strings broken and No 1 main rotor blade definitely not lined up where it ought to be. We add the tip socks, with two men on each, plug in a flight deck tractor and towing arm (the operator of which cheerfully claims that they usually break the tail wheel lock pin with this particular towing arm!) and King Kong's younger brother masquerading as an overzealous 'pinkie' (electronic maintenance rating) hell bent on tearing the radio fit out of the aircraft. Honestly, Fred Karno would have been in his element here.

With the Sea King now resting in the 'Graveyard', peace and tranquility is finally restored. A 'Red' phone call to Wings on Mum, who agrees that a first light slot is the best time to recover. Armed with call signs, ship positions, reassured that we will not have to fly through our two hour extension, and then showered and fed, sleep was next on the agenda, but the promised telephone wake up call at 0600 did not materialise. There is a 'phone in every cabin, each of which has a volume control on the bell which, if you are not aware of it, is guaranteed to be turned fully down. Not so for the American 'Son of Black Rod' who decided to audition for his father's job on my cabin door at 0630!

Quick bite to eat, arrange aircraft move, warn out with Air Ops, ensure passengers are on their way to the aircraft - we should still make the 0730 planned departure. No Form 700 (maintenance book), but no flight servicing planned other than a normal turn round. Should be OK, do what you can remember of essential component checks, compressor oil levels both down a bit, a pint needed in one and about three in the other, bit of a hot gas leak evident on the engine bay door, but not really serious enough - and so into the cockpit I go.

Funny, I pulled all the normal circuit breakers plus a few extras last night, but most have since been 'made'. However, aircraft now on its 'spot', so strap in, battery master switches on, then some guy wants to know how much fuel I want! Aircrewman helpfully suggest that it might be worth taking a bit extra as the jettison pipe is pouring fuel all over the flight deck! A few rude words as I unmake the jettison switches, find the fuel management switches in a totally illogical pattern of selections - as are several other engine function switches. Someone has been messing with my aeroplane, and this is turning into a nightmare! Memories of Flight Safety film which starts off with the pilot not getting his 'shake'. Hairs on back of neck now standing up and screaming. Cancel planned departure, get on 'Red phone' to Mum, ask for maintainers, Form 700, engine oil etc and make decision that there are *too many little things* adding up, therefore be pedantic and don't be pressured into anything. Now feeling self-righteous but rather professional.

Incoming 'Red phone' call points out that Mum will be four hundred miles away in about six hours time and there is no way of getting maintainers to me; oil on offer from *USS Very Big* is quite suitable for use in our engines, and by the way you *are* qualified to flight service the aeroplane aren't you? Can you make it?

Can I refuse? Of course not. Next deck slot is 1100 and somehow the aircraft is started and spread with an action replay in reverse of the previous night's exertions on the head, plus access panels being ripped off the bottom of the gearbox to get at the slip rings. I have done what I can remember of the full After and Before Flight Servicing Schedules and, reassured that the next planned maintenance op is only on the rescue hoist, we are ready for take off. Aircrewman asks if we can get a nav update. I know USS *Very Big* is VERY big, but when the update is received and differs by nine degrees of longitude from the position given by their Air Ops section only thirty minutes previously, one has to be impressed with her turn of speed! Or, seriously wary of her navigational abilities...

Eventually, by dint of some very accurate DR navigation and more than a little inspired guess work, we found the *en route* Royal Fleet Auxilliary ship for a refuel and subsequently found Mum as well. I didn't '*learn about flying from that*', but in one simple 'milk run', several factors were encountered which may amuse, horrify or (hopefully) stimulate discussion in various crewrooms and bars. In future, the only sort of 'milk run' I am going to be interested in is of the Moose* variety!

ALWAYS CHECK!

Lt Mike Tidd   **846 Sqn**   **1989**

Based at Tretten, just north of Lillehammer in Southern Norway, we operated up into the mountains with the Royal Marines and also provided the occasional assistance to the Norwegian civil community. As the Squadron Ops Officer I would occasionally bag for myself an interesting or unusual task that came in.

One day we received a request from the Norwegian Electricity Board to assist them in the recovery of a *Snowtrak* from a frozen lake. The driver had apparently misjudged the thickness of ice as he drove across it, and ended up swimming as his vehicle broke through the ice and sank. The Norwegians had managed to winch the vehicle back out of the lake, but needed our assistance to fly it back down out of the mountains to a repair base. The *Snowtrak* was 'assessed' as right on the limits of the *Sea King*'s lift capacity of 8,000 lbs, so I flew up single pilot, in a stripped-out aircraft, with the lightest aircrewman in the Squadron.

On arrival, we surveyed the vehicle and discovered that it was actually heavier than originally thought. The only way to lighten it further was to remove the tracks; after a long argument, the Norwegians finally agreed and took a chainsaw to them. With that accomplished, the Military Air Operations Team (MAOT) soon had the vehicle rigged for lifting and we got airborne and moved in for the pickup. It was obviously every bit as heavy as advertised, as only with absolute maximum power applied were we just able to get it airborne and then start off down out of the mountains.

Concentrating on keeping the aircraft and load steady as we flew down the valley, I reached across to the fuel panel to open the cross-feed cock to balance the fuel between forward and aft tanks. Now, due to an unfortunate piece of design, the *Sea King's* cross-feed cock was very close to the fuel shut-off cocks, one for each engine. Having flipped the switch, I was just about to take my hand away when it suddenly occurred to me that I hadn't *visually* checked that I had the right switch! Glancing across, I saw to my horror that my fingers were resting on the port engine fuel shut-off switch!

With my heart in my mouth, I very quickly returned the switch to the 'open' position - and then held my breath while I waited for the engine to flame-out. If it did, I would not be able to sustain flight, even at the most efficient flying speed; the re-lighting procedure would only be halfway through when we hit the ground! Needless to say, if it did run down I would have to jettison the underslung *Snowtrak*, which would have been mightily embarrassing, to say the least!

To my enormous relief, my luck held, both engines kept running and my aircrewman didn't notice. Much chastened, I carefully delivered the vehicle to the Norwegian repair base, refuelled and set off back to Tretten with my tail firmly between my legs...

A FISHY TALE

Lt Paul Morris   **826 Sqn**   **1991**

During the First Gulf War Campaign in 1991, I was serving with the RFA Support Unit (RFASU) onboard the RFA *Fort Grange*. During the time out in the Gulf we had aircraft from both 826 Sqn and 846 Sqn embarked – pingers and junglies working together, shock horror! This obviously caused friction due the fierce rivalry of the two fraternities, and things sometimes got a bit heated throughout the embarkation, with practical jokes being played to wind each other up on regular occasions. Eventually 846 Sqn were tasked to operate from ashore, leaving 826 to enjoy the delights of RFA life on their own. To alleviate some of the boredom, a couple of the 826 guys had taken up fishing, with varying degrees of success, but it filled the time quite nicely. 846 Sqn still came by occasionally, for mail and other essential stores. On one visit, the *Sea King 4* had to remain for a few hours, due to unserviceability I think.

About a week after the aircraft had left us, 826 Sqn received a parcel via special delivery from 846 Sqn, addressed to the Watch Chief. When it was opened, the office erupted and physical sickness became an immediate worry. The parcel contained a very old and putrid fish!

The 846 aircrew had been complaining of some very 'nasty and unusual' smells emanating from the rear of the aircraft and when they eventually persuaded the maintainers that it wasn't just the Aircrewman's personal health causing it, they took a look. They discovered a large fish which had been quietly festering away in the tail cone for almost a week, in temperatures of 40 degrees and over. Obviously realising that it was their 'pinger' brethren who had planted this rotting object, they put it in a box and sent it straight back!

UN 'PEACEKEEPING' IN BOSNIA

Lt Cdr Rick Jones   845 Sqn   1992

I deployed as a Flight Commander with 845 Naval Air Squadron, from RNAS Yeovilton to the Yugoslav Theatre of Operations, on 11 November 1992. The detachment consisted of four *Sea King HC4s*, approximately 100 personnel, including a Headquarters element of the Commando Helicopter Operations and Support Cell (CHOSC), and a Military Air Operations Team (MAOT), plus a total of 37 vehicles. It was anticipated at the time that 845's deployment in support of the United Nations Protection Force might continue a little beyond the original end date of May 1993, maybe 6 months more. It did actually keep going for over six years!

Into this cauldron of ethnic tension, 845 deployed with a clear mandate to provide Casualty Evacuation (CASEVAC) support for all UN Forces in the former Yugoslavia. We were to be totally non-political and neutral in every sense; we had no offensive role whatsoever. The squadron had not long before returned from what is now known as the 'first' Gulf war where many valuable lessons had been learned. In that conflict, aircraft self-defence and warning devices had been quickly cobbled together and then bolted on, to aid protection against a formidable perceived threat. After the hostilities we worked out which bits of kit we wanted and which we didn't, so that by the time we appeared in the Balkans, the enhancements included IR (Infra Red) missile jammers, MAWs (Missile Approach Warners) coupled to seductive flare launchers, (RWRs) Radar Warning Receivers, manual 'chaff' launchers - and makeshift armour-plated seats.

The aircraft had also been given a distinctive UN white paint scheme, and we were all given the individual extra protection afforded by the UN blue beret and badge! After 3 weeks of intensive negotiations ashore, the squadron disembarked from RFA *Argus* to its new home at Divulje Barracks, a former Yugoslavian Federal Army camp and heliport, partially laid waste by its former Serbian occupants and located 10 miles west of Split. At Divulje, 845 Sqn shared the heliport with a French unit operating *Puma* and *Gazelle*. Croatian aircraft, both helicopters and light fixed wing, were also based there.

The squadron complex (known as 'Steel City') comprised a range of largely purpose-built portakabins and ISO containers. These housed offices, stores and workshops to keep our aircraft going. We were positioned alongside the Royal Engineers' ISO park, but the big difference was we used initiative and native cunning to enhance our real estate - with a view to making it comfortable for 'round the clock' operations. The RFA's *Resource*, Sir *Bedivere* and latterly Sir *Percivale* – all garrison supply ships berthed in Split - were invaluable sources of both material and hospitality. We also became the proud owners of 2 fastbuild '*RUBB*' hangars (being built of rubber, of course), that afforded a high degree of weather protection for our aircraft.

Following arrival in Split on 19 November, 845 continuously maintained two aircraft at an hour's notice for CASEVAC tasking. However, the aircraft were only occasionally called upon to act in this role, and then only for non-combat casualties, which I must say pleased us at the time. Our aircraft were also fortunate to receive an excellent radar air traffic control and warning service from the orbiting 'Eye in the Sky' *AWACS* aircraft with their incredible airborne radar. Their radio call sign was '*MAGIC*' and they were too! Much of our flying was training, including Night Vision Goggle (NVG) sorties and mountain flying, using snow capped peaks up to 5500 feet in the local area and more than 7000 feet in Bosnia; SAR exercises; winching; load lifting and general flying practice to keep us current in a variety of roles. Additionally, we were able to practice instrument approaches to Split airport and complete NVG training for the majority of our first tour pilots, quickly bringing them up to operational status.

Our accommodation was a former barrack block, renamed '*The Sheraton*', which had undergone a near-total refurbishment in the hands of the 845 '*design, build and bodge as necessary*' team, again with great help from the RFA ships. After scrubbing out, re-painting, window repairs and much interior joinery we had the best living space anywhere around. The Wardroom, Senior and Junior Rates Messes were opened on the 21st December and were highly prized as havens of comfort and relaxation, and the envy of other troops who didn't have the 'get up and go' to help themselves. Sleeping areas in the block comprised 6 mess decks with 15 or more personnel in each. The once defunct central heating system was put into working order, though hot water for showers was a hit-or-miss affair; sea-shower economy routines were enforced - wet all over, stop flow - soap all over, the water on and quickly wash off. By comparison with the other British servicemen at Vitez and Tomislavgrad, and due entirely to our own efforts, our surroundings were comfortable and morale was high - despite having to spend Christmas and New Year away from our families.

That first detachment was the end of the quiet time for me, but I returned for a second tour, in mid Feb 93, to a totally different set of circumstances. On 24 Mar I flew a sortie from Split (a Croatian area) into Srebrenica to pull out a couple of individuals, with one night at the UN-occupied hotel 10 miles west of Sarajevo at Kiseljak, a Bosnian Muslim area. I had to sleep on the hotel floor after being briefed on the task, but got little sleep on my roll mat on the concrete surface! Left some of my kit in Kiseljak, thinking I'd be back in no time, then flew to Tuzla in North Bosnia – a Muslim area, leaving more kit there, to fly on to Zvornik, a Bosnian Serb area. In the process of crossing the Muslim / Serb line we landed at a football stadium and were checked out by Serbs, suspicious because of the areas we had come from. I have to say we had a nervous time, trying to explain away the contents of a survival pulk which had two cookers with solid fuel cartridges, complete with a poison sign on the packaging!

We were about to take off when some French *Pumas* appeared saying the landing site was being shelled, which didn't sound too good for our 'peaceful' mission! We therefore flew back to Tuzla where we heard that some Canadian UN soldiers in Srebrenica had been injured. George Wallace and Brian Smith (our 'tame Crab' exchange pilot on 845) flew in and winched them off the Post Office roof, that being the only safe place to effect the transfer. At Tuzla that night were 3 RN *Sea Kings*, 3 French *Pumas* and a French *Gazelle*. However, out of the frying pan and into the fire, as the saying goes, as we were then shelled by Serbs - so decided that jumping into the back of a *Warrior* Armoured Personnel Carrier was quite the best course of action, with the *Sea King* definitely not being armoured!

We then decided to stay, which proved to be a mistake - as snow clouds moved in, we couldn't fly and our main 'survival' kit was still in Kiseljak! We also discovered that the British Army were running out of food, which didn't sound too good, then had to sleep on the floor of a workshop, which was even worse! Also became aware that Muslim girls were doing the translating in exchange for food, and of course they were considerably hungrier than the British Army! We had a very boring time playing games for a while, but did then get thanked by General Morillon, the French Commander, who got us and the French aircrew together, to our mutual advantage. BBC's Kate Adie then turned up, which was a sure sign that more shelling was due!

On 25 March I crewed up with Andy Clarke to fly General Morillon to Kiseljak, but low cloud blocked us and we returned to Tuzla. During more shelling there we went into a 'reinforced' room in the main block where I tried to cheer up the 2 injured Canadian soldiers: *'Where are you from in Canada?'* (NW of Ottawa); *'Is it nice there?'* (No); *'What's it like in winter?'* (Cold) - and so on. I did chat about my wife being Canadian, a tenuous link with their vast empty country so many miles away, but not sure if I cheered them up at all! On the last morning we cleared the snow off rotor blades and fuselages, to find a few holes in the helicopters. On 28 Mar we finally got away, picked up our kit and spare crew at Kiseljak, then returned to Split to find one *RUBB* hangar had blown down in 80 knot winds.

On 4 Apr I flew a 5 hour rescue mission in company with Kev Smith. We went to Kiseljak (land/fuel) – Then Tuzla – To Zvornik (searched by Serbs again) – To Srebrenica (Muslim haven) – Back to Tuzla (land) and Kiseljak (land) - To Split. Flew across the Muslim / Serb boundary between Tuzla and Zvornik at 1500 feet – Kev Smith was at 1000 ft and got a bullet through his fuel tank. Could I come down to check it for any leaking? No, I could not, said I, but you could come up to *my* height! It didn't look too bad, so we continued to Srebrenica. There we found lots of people on the ground, fires in lots of the houses, all perched on steep sides of the valley and with power cables everywhere. Very difficult and cramped approach to a landing in a football field. A woman with child tried to rush the *Sea Kings* to dump her offspring in the back, to give it the chance of a better life - but we couldn't do it as we were there to lift out an injured BBC reporter and a few others, one a Muslim who had got out in a remote part of Tuzla airfield and

130

disappeared into the woods - just the kind of person that the very warlike Serbs must have been after.

19/20 Apr: A triple *SK4* move to Tuzla, then Srebrenica starting at 0900; total casevacs lifted on both days 481. Also moved 16 flexible fuel tanks to Kiseljak to meet a C130 *Hercules*, with fuel and a pump. 1 x RN fuel bowser was fixed and sent to Kiseljak as well. Despite having a fuel endurance of 6 hours, one of our big problems was lots of flying a long way from fuel sources, so we had been using French fuel. At Split I was in the Army HQ when Bianca Jagger asked me whether she could get to Tuzla with us – I suggested she try the French as her trip was not strictly 'operational' – she was trying to get a young girl out to hospital. One out of many thousands; I heard later that she had succeeded!

THE (Future) KING AND I

Lt Cdr Mike Abbey   CO 845 Sqn   1996

Earlier in this book I was a Sub-Lieutenant in 845, but I had started out as a fairly rare animal in those days, namely a front-line squadron *Midshipman*! I must have stayed out of trouble some of the time, because I fooled enough people to eventually get an appointment as Senior Pilot of 707, the Jungly training squadron, and in 1995 had somehow risen to the dizzy heights of Commanding Officer of 845. It is the sort of job that you always imagined older and more senior people doing, but here I was, actually in charge! In February 1996, two flights from my squadron, including me personally, were deployed to Split (known locally as 'NAS *Banana*' for obvious reasons.

This was just after the Dayton peace accord had been signed, which was intended to stop the war which Serbs and Croats had been fighting for some five years. Some bigwig decided a Royal Visit by the Prince of Wales was needed to show solidarity with our troops and raise their morale. Croats had moved out of the area of Sipovo, burning, looting and destroying everything as they went and the whole country looked a complete mess, rather like the aftermath of WW2; it was this area that HRH was to see.

We were tasked to pick the Prince of Wales up in Split,

direct from his Queen's Flight jet and take him to stay overnight in HMS *Illustrious*, the security situation being too dangerous for him to remain ashore. This plan was good in theory, unlike the weather which was awful and the night which was very *very* dark. We launched from Split with everyone in the back of the *Sea King* plugged in to their headset stations. Sometimes this can cause dreadful feedback and 'white noise', such that the pilot can't hear a thing. During the short trip, while on night vision goggles, the aircrewman was moving around the back like the road manager at a Glastonbury pop festival, unplugging and replugging each headset in turn to find the rogue electrical lead, but in this case unsuccessfully.

Up front, the co-pilot and I were working furiously to try and understand the ship's homing directions on the radio, all the while peering into the green-tinted gloom to try and catch sight of her. I have a hairy neck, and at about one mile range from the ship these hairs went a little berserk, so in reaction I looked down at the instrument panel to see the Radar Altimeter unwinding through 100 feet! Not so good, and very much lower than we should have been at that range AND going down rapidly, but in time I pulled full power and got us back up to where we ought to be!

Just after that I saw the ship's glideslope indicator; the bad dream was over. The following day we dropped the Prince at Split to be whisked off to Sarajevo in his jet, while we followed at a more sedate pace. After visiting troops there we were to take him to Maconichgrad to visit a Parachute Regiment unit who were busily attempting to make safe a large minefield. A RAF *Chinook* had been tasked to carry the remainder of his entourage, press people, military PR gurus, baggage etc - and they trailed along in our wake.

The weather looked very iffy indeed, with a frontal system, snow falling, low cloud, high winds and not a good forecast for the next 24 hours. However, Split to Sarajevo empty proved to be OK and after picking up the Prince, our journey over the lower ground on to Maconichgrad was adequate - and we made the landing on time, as ever, and much to the relief of the waiting Paras. The weather for the journey onwards through the mountains wasn't so good though; after lengthy discussions we worked out that the Prince was happy to stay overnight at Maconichgrad, and the local Regiment more than happy for him to stay. I told everyone concerned, very convincingly, that I absolutely did *not* want to be scrubbing along in amongst the weeds with my future King in the back etc. etc. having scared myself fartless only the night before!

In the way that these things often happen in the Military, common sense was there in adequate quantity, staring you in the face, but the decision was still made by 'a higher authority' (than the future King?) to go ahead with the programme as originally planned.

I then said: *"He has to be ready by 1600 or we'll be getting out of difficult, mountainous terrain in very poor weather, with the future King on board, in the bloody dark - and I'm not doing it!"* Everyone agreed this was a fine plan and we would do it. Miraculously, HRH turned up exactly on time. It does seem that if he had stayed he would have been in the middle of a known minefield overnight, which the higher authority wasn't too pleased about...

I took off with His Nibs in the back, the *Chinook* following in line astern with the 'also rans', but the *Royal Crab Force* then turned back at the first valley, which predictably was a bit full of snow storm. However, you can actually see *through* falling snow quite well, so I kept on going at below 100 ft in order to keep in contact with the visual references - as we had been taught to do so well at Bardufoss. I have to say it wasn't the hairiest weather I'd ever flown through, but not at all nice and in retrospect, I may have done very badly at my Court Martial if it had all gone wrong. I did wonder in an idle moment if they could revert me as far down as Midshipman again.

HRH was standing between the front seats, chatting amicably to the pair of us, including reminiscing about his days as a Jungly, which he had obviously thoroughly enjoyed. About 30 minutes after take-off and having done some reasonably demanding 'pressing on' - when we should perhaps have not pressed at all - we popped out of a valley into the most beautiful crystal clear weather imaginable, on the other side of the weather front. The contrast was stunning and we all marvelled in the beauty of the moment, even though it was still a bit windy. We now had to focus on another problem of the region, which included climbing to get out of range of hostile small arms - which was quite important (now that they could see us), because they did shoot at us quite often!

Then, while we were in a climb and going through 2,500 feet we hit the most monumental standing wave, which happens when the air mass follows an orographic feature (the mountain), up and down in a lovely smooth and uniform wave. We rose like a cork from a champagne bottle in the upflow, such that with the lever fully down, i.e. in autorotation, we were going up at 2,000 ft per minute.

Needless to say, what goes up must come down - and about two minutes after getting lifted bodily upwards, the reverse happened and despite full power from both engines we plummeted earthwards at a 2,000 ft per minute rate of descent. The funny bit though was the change-over between up and down, when the aircraft became effectively weightless. Spookily, I looked over my shoulder at precisely the correct moment and saw, rather like in an astronaut's training aircraft, the future King floating in mid air for a good few seconds, hanging on for dear life to the front seats before coming back to earth/cabin floor with a bit of a crash!

It was at this point that I got all responsible and invited him to go back and strap in. My Midshipman's uniform stayed in the loft, thank goodness!

JUNGLIES IN THE DESERT

TO IRAQ AND BACK

Lt Cdr Rich Harrison   **845 NAS**   **2003**

My first experience of Iraq was on the night of 20 March 2003 when I led a formation of *Sea King 4s* filled with Royal Marines into the Al Faw peninsula, on the south-eastern tip of Iraq. I had recently returned to 845, having just completed training as a Helicopter Warfare Instructor (HWI). When I rejoined, the prospect of conflict with Iraq was gaining momentum and as the HWI I was responsible for ensuring that all aircrew were trained in the tactical aspects of operating the *SK4*. It was likely to be a very hostile environment, so I was a very busy chap for the few months leading

134

up to the invasion...

The goal of course was to topple Saddam Hussein and in the days prior to the assault, 845 Sqn was camped out in the deserts of Kuwait, standing by for instructions to carry out the mission. These were tense times, with lots of waiting around, enduring unpleasant sandstorms and making final checks of the carefully rehearsed plan. Every so often, air raid warnings in the form of Land Rover horns sounding urgently would send us diving into fox holes, throwing on our respirators (gas masks), never knowing if it was for real or just another false alarm. Anxieties were heightened because it was known the Iraqis had a proven capability to use chemical or biological weapons against us. Even though we were well informed and trained in this aspect of warfare, the prospect was daunting.

When finally given the order to launch, we did so with considerable confidence in our training, planning and tactical ability as a force. We had particularly good intelligence on the number of enemy facing us at the chosen objectives, and while we anticipated a stiff fight we were glad to have the support of A10 ground attack and C130 *Minigun* aircraft to provide cover in the event of resistance. As we flew over the border, low level and at night using Night Vision Goggles (NVG), the prospect of being engaged by missiles, anti-aircraft guns or small arms fire was very real. After aborting the first insertion attempt because of an enemy mortar attack at the landing site, my section dropped our troops at the objective, luckily without mishap or casualty.

Once key oil installations and infrastructures on the Al Faw peninsula had been secured, troops of 3 Commando Brigade and the Queen's Dragoon Guards advanced towards Basra, supported by *Sea King*, *Lynx* and *Gazelle* helicopters of the Commando Helicopter Force. For the next two weeks I flew some very long and unglamorous missions supporting the ground troops with re-supplies of ammunition, food, water and even fresh laundry! Very quickly, the city and airport to its north west were secured and we set up an operating base at the airfield.

I recall in those last weeks wondering what would happen now that the dictator had been toppled. The local population showed a range of emotions at our presence, some jubilant and friendly, others suspicious and even frightened. Our main focus

135

seemed to be establishing security in the region and allowing things to settle down in their own good time.

After the 4 month deployment I returned home just in time to witness the birth of my first child, and my personal focus was now very much directed towards fatherhood. At work I was appointed to a Commando Helicopter Tactical Development desk job at the Maritime Warfare Centre. Part of my work was to maximise the protection afforded to helicopters against missile threats in Iraq; I returned to the country following the tragic loss of an 847 Sqn *Lynx* in 2006. During the 6 weeks I then spent in theatre, it was clear that the Iraq I had returned to had changed considerably.

Insurgents were now actively targeting coalition forces in the provinces of South Eastern Iraq. Helicopters were extremely busy providing a life-saving Incident Response Capability, the military equivalent of Search and Rescue and Air Ambulance, to troops on the ground. The threat to all military helicopters had increased considerably and they were now being regularly engaged by hostile enemy fire as they carried out their daily tasks. Aircrew were under no illusions as to what would happen if they were shot down and captured by insurgent forces.

The final and most notable difference was that the insurgents were actively targeting Basra Air Base, home to over three thousand British troops, with rocket and mortar attacks. Even behind the security fences no-one was safe. This fact became particularly apparent during my final tour of Iraq in the summer of 2007 after I had rejoined 845 in the post of Detachment Commander in theatre. Rocket attacks against the base had become an occupational hazard, happening several times a day and usually in salvos of 4 or 5. On one occasion a salvo of 17 rockets landed in the base over a period of a few minutes and as I lay in the sand, face down I wondered if it would ever stop! On another occasion I was walking across dispersal to my aircraft when the alarm sounded and rockets rained down all around me with deafening explosions as I hugged the red-hot tarmac.

In June 2007 we suffered more rocket attacks in one month than had been the case for the entire year of 2006, a single statistic that demonstrated just how much more intense the level of insurgency had become. Tragically, several British servicemen were killed by these attacks in the twelve weeks I was there. Similarly British troops at Basrah Palace in the City were regularly targeted by mortars and ambushed by Improvised Explosive Devices, small arms and rockets whilst out on patrol. When I finished my tenure as Detachment commander, Basra Palace was handed over to Iraqi authorities and a temporary lull in the level of insurgent attacks gave the impression of calm and security.

I returned to the UK, glad to be away from the 50 deg heat and featureless brown landscape, allowing me a temporary return to normal before I re-deploy to Afghanistan in Spring 2008, for more adventures in the sun and sand.

TANK BUSTING IN IRAQ

Lt Cdr James Newton DFC   847 Sqn   2004
This extract is from Jim Newton's excellent book 'ARMED ACTION'

Strictly speaking, the role of 847 in Iraq was to act as a 'screen' in conjunction with the armoured reconnaissance vehicles below, observing enemy positions and then calling in fire from the Royal Marine artillery on the ground, or from the guns on the Royal Navy frigates and destroyers, or from the fast jet boys thousands of feet above our heads, returning from missions deep in Iraq. We were not meant to go into offensive mode unless there was no alternative, or unless one of our TOW missiles was the most appropriate weapon for the task in hand. Held in our battle position (BP) as we were, there was, on this occasion, clearly no alternative if we were to come under fire. It was a *battle*.

I was talking to Geek in the *Gazelle*, the other helicopter in our 847 air patrol – who, like me, was scanning the date palms with his sight – when a shell exploded about 400 metres behind us. Four hundred metres may sound like a long way, but in a tank battle it is a bit close for comfort.

"Aye, aye, this is getting pretty warm," I said to Gizmo, who was flying our aircraft; he just nodded back at me, looking totally unbothered. He might as well have been deadheading roses back in the West Country. Barely had the words left my mouth when there was a second, much louder explosion, this time around 200

metres behind us and a thirty-foot geyser of sand and smoke shot into the air. The first, I suspected, had just been a random shot into the desert, but the second blast made me seize my controls, partly because of the shock of the explosion itself, but more because I understood instantly that a second shot along exactly the same angle, so quickly following the first, could mean only one thing: an Iraqi tank commander had us in his sights, and he was rapidly adjusting fire.

We didn't want to break away too hard because it was vital to get 'eyes on' the tank and then take it out, and in order to get eyes on we had to try and hold the hover position so I had a good stable view in the sight. So Gizmo took our *Lynx* drifting to the right as I carried on frantically looking up and down the date palms for the camouflaged tanks, which can be difficult to spot at the best of times, let alone when they are operating from under a uniform line of trees in a heat haze.

"It's like looking for a needle in a haystack," I muttered into my boom mike. We had moved a few hundred metres to the east and returned to the hover, still only about fifty feet above the ground, when a third round erupted right in front of us and the heady stench of explosive instantly filled the cockpit. Gizmo and I shot looks at each other, both knowing exactly what was going on. He was bracketing us. He'd put two rounds over the top and one in front and now all he had to do was slightly adjust the elevation and lob one down the middle and we were as good as dead...

I had trained for this moment on countless occasions in recent years, but this guy was running rings around me. I hadn't got the faintest idea where he was firing from. He, meanwhile, was just a few yards, and a few seconds, from blowing us out of the sky. We might as well have been strapped to the end of his barrel. I could picture perfectly the scene going on in the Russian-built *T55*. The commander would be barking orders and range adjustments at his gunner below, while sticking out of the turret and looking down his own sights, with us sitting slap-bang in the crosshairs of his graticule.

Like me, he had high-magnification sights and I knew he would be looking right at my desperate face as I scrutinised the horizon to find him. This guy knew his stuff, and it was bloody obvious what was coming next – airburst. He was implementing basic anti-aircraft tactics: get your range with point detonation rounds and then switch to airburst, which is basically 'ack-ack', or *flak*, which armies have been using to bring down aircraft since the First World War. It was so bloody hot in the midday sun that sweat was running down my face and into my eyes, and I was wiping it away with my sleeve so that I could see through the sights, when there was an ear-splitting bang to the rear of the aircraft. Even Gizmo, a Royal Marine veteran, raised an eyebrow at that one and we both instinctively knew that it was time to move – and fast.

Gizmo broke hard to the right and we sped towards the back of our battle box as I tried to gather my thoughts and work out what to do. There was only one way of getting out of there intact and that was to find the tank – or tanks – firing at us, and then take them out with a TOW. I had never fired a TOW in anger, let alone killed anyone. Although I had scored two direct hits out of two during training in Oman on the way out to the Gulf, these missiles from the Vietnam era had an unpleasant but rare habit of 'roguing' on us.

Both helicopters made two laps around our battle box, each time searching for the tiny pinprick muzzle flashes amid the date palms as we sped towards the enemy. But to no avail; there was still no sign of him. We tried the 'split' manoeuvre next, whereby the two helicopters raced towards the treeline side by side and then split, one banking left and one banking right, hoping the tank would be confused about which one of us to fire at, leaving one aircraft 'engaged' and the other free to help. The air was full of drifting smoke and puffs of airburst explosion as the Iraqis continued to fire at us for fun, pumping out shell after shell, one every five seconds. By the law of averages alone, this guy was due a hit sooner or later. He deserved one, too, because so far at least he was completely manoeuvring and outfoxing us.

"*Geek, this is Scooby...*" I said, calling up the *Gazelle*.

"*Go!*" replied Geek.

"*Where is this guy?*" I said as the airbursts rained down on us.

"*Er ... no tally...*" came the reply, meaning that he couldn't see him either. "*Do you want us to push forward and have a look for him, Scooby?*"

To find this tank we would have to get up as close as

possible to his rough location - and stay in the hover. To be honest, when it comes to being shot out of the sky, there's not much difference between being one kilometre away or five kilometres. They're just numbers. If the tank commander has you in his sights and you're within the range of his gun, then it makes little odds. My survival instinct was telling me to retreat the four kilometres to the back of our box, but the chances of spotting the tanks from so far back were much smaller. We had to get in there.

Gizmo pushed right up to within a few hundred metres of the front of the battle box, and we had only just gone into the hover when there was a loud crash a little to our right, followed immediately by what felt like a huge sack of gravel being thrown over the right-hand window… One, two, three, four, five - *BOOM!* Another blinding flash lit up the air in front of us, at our eleven o'clock: the explosion so strong I could feel my armoured chest plate lift away from my body and the *Lynx* bucked wildly as if a lorry had just rammed into us at speed. At the same time a deluge of what sounded like giant hailstones crashed against the windscreen and the helicopter quickly filled with the stench of cordite again.

"Scooby section, break right! Break right!" I yelled, ordering both aircraft to move. But I didn't need to tell Gizmo. He was already putting the *Lynx* into a hard manoeuvre, which was just as well, because a third airburst immediately erupted into the space we had just vacated, once again causing the helicopter to lurch and jolt as we veered away. As we were speeding away from the immediate danger, a quiet voice spoke in my headset:

"Excuse me, boss…"

It was Guns, the marine door-gunner in the back of the *Lynx*. I had almost forgotten about the young lad amid all the excitement of being blown to shit by an unsighted enemy.

"What's up, Guns?" I said, almost impatiently.

"Well, boss, I don't know whether you're interested, but I've just seen a muzzle flash…"

I swung round in my seat to see Guns down on one knee, leaning on his mounted machine gun looking – well, looking quite bored really, like he was off in Dreamland, making his holiday plans or thinking about his girlfriend.

"Interested!?! I'm fascinated! You may just have saved our lives.

Where the hell is it? And try and look a little bit flustered or excited, will you, Guns? We're in a battle..."

"No bother, boss..."

Gizmo was moving the *Lynx* all around the box, desperately trying to disrupt the tank gunner's line and range, but now we swept back in towards the date palms as Guns started talking us on to the muzzle flash he had spotted: 'From the cream building come right two fingers (ie the width of two fingers held out in front of my face), low apex building with no front. Got it? Keep coming right, boss, keep coming right, that's it, just in there, boss, by the building?' He was virtually yawning. My heart leapt with relief and excitement as I finally laid eyes on our tormentor.

There he was, not right in front of us at all, but out on our nine o'clock, over to the left. No wonder I couldn't find him. The bastard had outflanked us, which is exactly what you didn't want in a helicopter because you're generally moving forward and looking down the sight ahead of you. As he was firing at us from side-on, he also had a much bigger target to hit. This guy was no rookie fresh out of tank college, that was for sure; he was a pro, probably a vet of the first Gulf War or the long conflict with Iran. He was brave too, because he had obviously broken cover and come right out of the date palms to engage us. So far as I could tell, the rest of them had stayed put.

"I've got it! I've got it!" I blurted out as I caught sight of a minuscule white flash. Almost immediately there followed the mother of an explosion right in front of us that made the *Lynx* jerk violently as Gizmo wrestled to regain control. The bad news was that the tank was sitting inside the open end of what looked distinctly like some kind of school, because it had a kind of concourse playing area out the front. Crafty bastard, this one. Just as it was not great PR to shoot up an ambulance, neither would it look too great if I called in a bombing strike, or fired in a load of TOWs and wiped out a classroom of five-year-olds.

I put the sight on visual, to its highest magnification, and then switched to thermal imaging, just to make absolutely certain – and, thankfully, it was obvious there were no people inside the building that day. All the same, the Iraqi authorities could still use the images of shattered desks as a powerful piece of propaganda. They could be beaming them around the world by the time we

141

landed back at base. As we swung round and I fixed the building in my sights, it was clear that in order to fire at us, the tank was having to drive out of the school and then quickly reverse back in - before we could spot him. When he next sped out into the open to have a pop at us, that was going to be my window of opportunity. It was a small one, but it was at least a chance.

This was now a classic tank engagement - a straight gunfight. The best shot would win. The loser would die in flames. I wasn't thinking in human terms; it was helicopter versus tank. The training had kicked in, and it was as if I had been pre-programmed to delete any thoughts about fellow souls. All I could see was 60 tons of Russian armour. The tank commander would have been in the same mindset; for him, it was just tank versus helicopter. Exhilaration had now replaced the fear and frustration that had gripped me for the past thirty minutes. The *Gazelle* moved to the relative safety of the back of the battle box to watch our six o'clock. I needed Geek to get word back to HQ that developments on the battlefield were moving fast. There was nothing that the unarmed '*whistling chicken leg*', as we called the *Gazelle*, could bring to the battlefield now that we had our target. And it was perfectly clear that it was the bigger beast of the *Lynx* that this guy wanted as his trophy. With all our explosives on board, we'd make a far more satisfying bang than the little *Gazelle*...

There were two problems, however. First, the tank was partly obscured in its hiding place and difficult to identify positively. This meant that there was a chance, albeit a small one, that it might have been a friendly, perhaps one of the Queen's Dragoon Guards *Scimitars* we were there to support. The last thing I needed was the first missile of my first war to take out some of our own boys. Second, it was sitting in an American-controlled zone and I would need to get the Yanks' permission to cross over to their patch to get a shot at it.

Perhaps sensing that we had finally spotted him, the tank commander opened up with a sustained volley of shells that erupted all around our airspace. How none of them had hit us yet was a miracle. I knew from our training over the years that, by rights, we should now be lying in a mangled, charred heap in the sand. Certainly, if this had been the Norwegian lads whom we'd trained against, it would have been all over after a couple of minutes. But our good fortune couldn't last forever.

As Gizmo banked and dipped and lifted to try and avoid the endless barrage of incoming flak, I was desperately working the radios to raise the American controllers for clearance to cross boundaries into their area of operation and take a shot. *'Come on, come on, will you?'* I muttered under my breath as I kept the sights glued to my face. Finally – probably after no more than thirty seconds in truth – the radio crackled into life and I heard that lazy Deep South drawl: *"Hello, Cravat 33, you're clear to proceed, but better get on with it. We have trade of our own..."*

I immediately switched frequencies to talk to the QDG to make absolutely certain it was not one of them sitting in there. The doubt in my mind was minuscule, but I didn't want there to be any doubt at all. I don't think I could fly again after a blue-on-blue incident. I put out a request for them to confirm it wasn't one of their tanks and one by one the Welsh boys came back over the airwaves: *"Zero One, negative… Zero Two, negative… Zero Three, negative… Zero Four negative..."* I was good to go.

"Roger that - firing..." I said into the radio, letting the QDG know that we were about to engage.

I selected the first TOW missile as we retreated to the back of the battle position, ready to turn and make a run for the tank. Taking a running shot at him was one option, but the chances of a direct hit were far greater if we closed in fast and then assumed the hover position, giving me a more solid platform to get the crosshairs on him before pulling the trigger. I would also have to hold the crosshairs on the target until the moment of impact, and that's easier if you're not hammering along at 100 knots and turning away at the same time.

The cat-and-mouse game of the last half-an -hour was now over. It was time for the *Lynx* to bare her claws. I felt a huge surge of adrenaline as Gizmo banked hard to the right, trimmed the cyclic forward and began to accelerate rapidly towards the tank, which was still pumping out round after round at us. I barely noticed the airbursts any longer as I focused all my concentration on putting the tank into the middle of the graticule and getting the missile away.

When we were about 3,500 metres from our target, Gizmo brought the Lynx to the hover and put it into 'constraints', the pre-programmed flying parameters within which the computer allows the missile to launch. I saw the tank muzzle flash as I squeezed the trigger; we were both firing simultaneously. Our shots would be crossing in mid-air. The TOW flopped out of its tube to the right of the aircraft; I watched its motor furiously burning itself out and felt its heat on my cheeks. The tank commander, seeing the bright flash, would have known exactly what was heading his way.

The motor burnt for about a second and a half before the missile raced away at about 700 mph into the distance, with its two copper guidance wires attached to the *Lynx*, spooling out of its arse. Gripping the TOW controller in my right hand until my knuckles were white, I held the crosshairs on the tank, tracking it all the way, as Gizmo counted the seconds before impact: '*eight, nine, ten …*' I held my breath as the sweat cascaded down my forehead. If we were buffeted by an explosion or a gust of wind, shunting the sight off the tank, the missile could go anywhere, or it could still 'rogue' and either flop into the sand or blast into the distance and cause horrible damage somewhere else, possibly to an innocent target.

It was just a matter of seconds, but the wait was interminable as the TOW rocketed at a slightly downward gradient towards the tank and Gizmo held the *Lynx* in post-launch 'constraints', which meant making sure not to turn the aircraft more than 110 degrees from the target. The tension was broken by a comic moment – almost surreal given the intensity of the situation – when one of the QDG tanks came over the radio: '*Hello, Cravat 33, this is Zero Five,*' said the Welsh accent. '*Well, don't ask me if I'm in that building then, will you boss?*'

Bollocks! I thought there were just four *Scimitars*, but having seen the T55 now with my own eyeballs, I knew for certain it was *not* a 'friendly' down there watching the TOW streak towards him. I laughed nervously at the comment, but the sound was barely out of my throat when a great flash filled the sight I was staring down.

"…. *Twenty, twenty-one, twenty-two* …. "continued Gizmo. Given the range, the fact he was still counting indicated that I had missed the target. I couldn't believe it. My heart sank heavily. Almost simultaneously another blast rocked the *Lynx* and another shower of gravel crackled again the windscreen.

I shouted out: "*The next round's for us, Gizmo, let's move!*"

Quickly we banked left – and the *Lynx* jolted as that next round exploded behind the tail rotor. He didn't say anything, but I could feel Gizmo's disappointment as we retreated to the back of the box. *"Right, this time we're doing a running shot. Let's get close, Gizmo,"* I said. The *Lynx* surged forward again, as Gizmo pushed it to about 100 knots, which was well short of the 247 mph the *Lynx* hit to set the world speed record for a helicopter, but about as fast as it would ever go in these conditions.

I pressed the button to cut the wires from the first missile and quickly primed a second one. I could now see that the first shot had landed about fifty metres short; it wouldn't have even singed the commander's eyebrows. The explosion, however, had obviously put the shits up him because he had darted back into the building like a rat down a drain and was now firing like a psycho from inside the concourse with everything he had left.

"You'd think this lad would be out of rounds by now..." said Gizmo as we sped back in, the blur of the desert rushing beneath us, like someone had pressed fast forward on the video recorder. I fixed the gap between the turret and the main body in the crosshairs and when we were about three kilometres away, I squeezed the trigger and waited. Gizmo started counting again, *"One, two, three…"*

It wasn't a big explosion like the first – just a small flash as the warhead penetrated the tank's armour. All the exploding was going on inside as the molten copper bolt bounced around the walls. After a few seconds there was a secondary explosion and smoke started pouring out of the turret as a figure jumped out and into the sand. *"Bullseye!"* said Geek, who had been watching the engagement from the back of the battle position in the *Gazelle*. There was no joy, only relief, as I sank back into my seat – but then, just when Gizmo started manoeuvring to turn us around, we were both thrown forward as the tank's parting shot exploded metres in front of us. It was the closest one yet. The compression waves lifted my chest armour off, winding me for a second time that day as the nose of the *Lynx* reared up in the turbulence.

"Right, we're bingo (low on fuel); let's get the hell out of here now, can we?" I said to Gizmo as he brought the aircraft back under control. He replied: *"That's not a bad idea - besides, I'm getting hungry.'*

145

It took about fifteen minutes to get back to the camp from the front line and we flew there in virtual silence. My hands were shaking so much I sat on them so that Gizmo wouldn't notice. We looked at each other and blew out our cheeks. Gizmo didn't say anything, but he gave me a look and a half-smile that spoke far more powerfully than any words - they said 'don't worry, Scooby, you're all right, you're not *meant* to feel relaxed...'

I was happy and relieved that my missile had eventually hit the target, but it was Guns who had saved our lives.

"Nice work, Guns..." I said over the comms.

"No bother, boss. I knew you'd get the bugger in the end -"

I craned my neck around to give the young lad a nod of thanks and congratulations and there he was, sitting at his door, one hand on the machine gun, legs dangling in the wind, like a bored kid killing time on the school wall - whistling.

BAPTISM OF FIRE

Lt Bridget Compain   **846 Sqn**   **2006**

Ladies arrived in Fleet Air Arm flying overalls in the 1990's; there are now a significant number of female Royal Navy officers flying as Pilots or Observers, and at present three are pilots in the Commando Squadrons. They go to the front line where they face identical risks and dangers as their male colleagues, while living in the same harsh field conditions.

Along with my husband, I transferred into the 'Andrew' from the Royal New Zealand Air Force; he came from the decline of our fast-jet world, from A4 *Skyhawks* to the *Sea Harrier*, while I left UH1 *Iroquois* helicopters for the Jungly world. We were going somewhat against the grain in making the move this way, because the more normal relocation for aircrew is from the British Isles to the Antipodes.

I arrived at Britannia Royal Naval College Dartmouth in January 2003 for my tailor-made (*'just cuff it'*!) RN familiarization training, and spent a few weeks discovering ships, cleaning duties and learning how to salute in a different way. Naturally, I received all the standard banter for being a former 'Crab' - and a *'Kiwi* Crab' as well - and now as a 'Wafu'!   I was then sent onward to commence flying duties, first to RAF Shawbury to do some flying with 705 Sqn in the AS350 *Squirrel,* purely to acclimatise me to the UK's flying rules and regulations. The *Squirrel* was a thrill to fly and I left Shawbury able to navigate without 10,000 ft mountains to help me, and also low fly - despite the lack of sheep for height judgment - a standard technique used in NZ for low-level work!

I then joined 848 NAS for Aircraft and Operational Conversion onto the *Sea King HC 4,* and found it a busy course with some extremely enjoyable flying. I developed a great admiration for the *SK4* and we organised some wonderful trips, such as a continental navigation to Italy for mountain flying. This type of sortie is very valid these days, as long range transcontinental deployments by air are often required.

My Royal Navy 'Wings' were presented on completion of the 848 course and I was appointed immediately to 846 Naval Air Squadron. My first two operational tours were to Bosnia Herzegovina, based at Banja Luka Metal Factory. Our main tasking was ferrying people to meetings, which in itself was monotonous, however it was a spectacular place to get airborne, which more than compensated for any boredom. However, the wires are another story as, scarily, they cross every flight path, with some spanning valleys 500 feet above the valley floor. Most crews experienced near misses at some point, me included, and following a *Lynx* wire strike that destroyed the aircraft, my respect for electricity cables became deeply ingrained...

This was the first time I had operated jointly with other nations, flying closely alongside the Romanians and their *Cougars* (super *Pumas*). They had many differing operational procedures and we learned that the definition of fancy dress could also vary a lot - we turned up to the party as mermaids, the Romanians simply wore their jeans back to front! I was regularly crewed up with a fellow female pilot and the reactions on troops' faces could be quite amusing when they realized two women were in control of this 21,000lb helicopter. Some would smile nervously and stare, others were truly petrified!

During these Bosnian tours we were fortunate enough to have spare time to explore, going for runs through the hills and local villages and into the cities for sightseeing and sampling local food and wine. I managed to get out with Liaison Officers to meet locals and spend time in different towns, while a few managed to get skiing (no off piste due to mines!); the battlefield tour of Sarajevo was also enlightening.

After 13 years of Junglies being in theatre, in March 2005 the Army Air Corps arrived to take the weight and we flew the *Sea Kings* home over three days, via Prague and Amsterdam. It was certainly a loss for the Multi-National Division, but an enjoyable finish to the tour for us. As for the operational element, Bosnia was a pleasant and gentle introduction for what was to come.

My next three tours were to be Op *Telic*, in Iraq. The *Tristar* flight into Basra initially seemed as if it could be a standard airline flight anywhere. It then became slightly alarming as everyone onboard put on helmets and body armour, then the aircraft went into blackout and spiral-dived toward the airfield. Not quite your standard holiday destination arrival.

I enjoyed my first Iraq tour, being a new theatre with novel things to see and experience, though the desert is a hard environment to operate in. Over the summer months we were flying in temperatures up to an unpleasant 50 deg C. Navigation in the desert can be demanding, with few features to give the normal cues so it was back to basic techniques, or more commonly 'thank you GPS!'. Much of the tasking involved flying long stretches of the country, which saw some very enjoyable low flying, often encountering large herds of camels. There are also many marsh areas, where pelicans and water buffalo were a regular sight, alongside the Marsh Arabs in their small boats. When flying across the desert it was a surprise to see Bedouin camps and these nomads roaming the desert, miles from anywhere. We would often receive waves from people, but we would also sometimes have bricks thrown and small arms fired at us.

We worked a rotating duty routine; rolling through tasking, test flights and incident response. Tasking was anything from 'bus runs', troop moves, Eagle Vehicle Check Points, top cover and reconnaissance. A fair amount of tasking was top cover for convoy moves and covering the many unfortunate roadside explosions. Formation night troop inserts were a highlight and we had a lot of success in many arrest operations. During reconnaissance missions I learnt what it was like to be a 'bagger' (AEW radar *Sea King*) sitting at altitude in a very boring hold pattern observing the ground, albeit the successful raids made it all worthwhile. We held an Incident Response Team (IRT) at immediate readiness in both Basrah and further North at Al Amarah. This consisted of the aircrew, two medics and a team of four Airborne Reaction Force (ARF) troops, who came along to provide security for the aircraft and medics at landing sites.

IRT was the most intense flying of all, more often than not for serious incidents and always time critical. We regrettably had many IRT accounts to talk about, one of which tells the story of a *Sea King* called out after a ground patrol came into contact with insurgents, to pick up an Army lad who had his leg blown off by a RPG (Rocket Propelled Grenade). Once he was in the aircraft, the crewman put a headset on him to let him speak to the medics, but his initial words to the crew were: "*I'm so sorry; I hope you didn't have to get out of bed for this...*"

We worked hard, and any down time could be spent in the on-camp cafés, the internet or in the '*Camels Toe*' bar. Accommodation was a set of 'temporary' seven man tents; after years of use the fabric is still apparently mortar and rocket proof! At Al Amarah we worked out of hardened accommodation, supplied with a multitude of nasties. One evening a camel spider held me hostage in the shower block for an hour. So my three tours in Iraq were an excellent 'experience', the flying good and operations very rewarding. It was a diverse deployment; the squadron personnel pulled together to do a fantastic job in an awful environment.

On return from Iraq I deployed to Bardufoss, North Norway - a temperature change of 80 degrees C. The *Sea Kings* were carrying out winter training there, but I went only to complete the Arctic survival course, in preparation for flying in the coming months. Although it is an extremely harsh environment to operate in, the Junglies have been training at Bardufoss since 1969. Norway has a remarkable landscape, but aside from freezing in my snow hole, it was extremely enjoyable.

When the Israel/Lebanon crisis occurred in July 2005 there were rumours we might be sent and a 'just in case' line was drawn on a map joining up necessary fuel stops etc. A few days later at 11am we were told, 'we're briefing at 2pm for a 3pm launch'. We all promptly raced home to re-pack our body armour and sunscreen before returning to the Squadron to sort out the finer details. In an astonishing effort by all, our six aircraft formation did indeed launch at 3pm en-route to Akrotiri, Cyprus – where we would be based for Op *Highbrow*. It took us two days and 20 hours flying to reach Akrotiri, via various stops across Europe. When we arrived, the evacuation of nationals was almost complete, done mostly by RN ships. Nevertheless the *Sea Kings* were utilised for passenger and troop moves into Beirut and the whole deployment was an incredible feat for six aircraft and their crews at such short notice.

In September my flight deployed to HMS *Ocean* and joined the amphibious task force for the Exercise *Vela* deployment. This involvd training for our taskforce and carrying out joint exercises with the Sierra Leone Armed Forces. With the focus having been predominantly ashore in Iraq for the past two years, it had been some time since we had got back to our core roots of amphibious tasking. The work-up took place off the South West coast of England where we were re-acquainted with ship-borne flying and working with a Commando of Royal Marines. For most, the littoral environment was a welcome change of scenery before setting set sail for Sierra Leone, Africa, via a long weekend stop in Gibraltar.

It was hard to believe what the country had endured in recent years, while flying over its vast expanse of jungle and tropical beaches. We were fortunate on jungle survival not to encounter many of the poisonous creatures we were repeatedly warned about, although the balance of Nature was restored when the heavens opened and it rained torrentially all night.

The 'Tailored Air Group' (TAG) embarked in HMS *Ocean* is made up of our 845/846 Sqn *Sea Kings*, 847 *Lynx* and 820 *Merlins*. Many of us, particularly the Jungly element, realized how little exposure we'd had to Naval operations recently and thoroughly enjoyed the amphibious environment. We kept a busy programme going with troop moves, load lifting, amphibious offloads and utilising the many secondary roles such as fast roping, helicopter In Flight Refuelling, hi-line transfers, winch transfers and casevacs. It was also good to learn first hand about the roles of the 'grey' *Merlins* which I had little experience of.

The locals proved to be inquisitive and very welcoming as

we worked up toward the final 'live exercise' which culminated in a Commando group assault. It was an eventful exercise, followed by the always enjoyable self-deployed flight home.

My time on 846 NAS has been remarkably varied; in just over two years I have deployed to Bosnia, Iraq, Norway, Cyprus, Sierra Leone and from HMS *Ocean*. In the space of a few months, the Squadron and ever-durable *Sea King* 4s have operated in temperate, desert, arctic and jungle environments and although the helicopter is now 28 years old, she's maintained well and continues to soldier on. As with every unit, there are things Junglies could do better, but we continue to be professional, work hard and as I'm sure any of the troops we support will vouch, we do an excellent job.

My next appointment is to the Qualified Helicopter Instructor Course at the Central Flying School, after which I will be back at 848 Naval Air Squadron, teaching a new generation of Junglies!

EMERGENCY GPS LET DOWN

Lt 'Logie' Baird   **846 NAS**   **2006**

I was part of the joint 845/846 Squadron detachment that formed the Commando Helicopter Force Iraq, or CHF(I), which had been operating from Basrah since 2003 and to a large extent viewed the place as 'home from home.' This detachment had a more diverse role than that of the traditional Jungly squadron in that much of its tasking was covert - and at night.

This particular day started as normal, with the squadron brief at 1630, to cater for our predominantly nocturnal existence in Operation Telic. The Met man stated that there would be fog forming, but it wasn't expected until around 0200. My planned landing time was 2300, so no real problem there. We crew-briefed at 1730, with a planned take-off time of 1900, and when we walked out to the aircraft at 1825 we checked the Met again, but no change. However, recognising the fact that the mission might alter and the fog could just be a bit early, I elected to increase the fuel load, giving us an additional 25 minutes endurance.

The first two hours of the sortie were dedicated to a familiar and frequent task, but as the third hour began we were warned for a high priority mission to the south of Basrah, where a strike operation was being considered for later on that night. Our operating altitude was to be high level. It was at about this time that the weather on the ground started to get worse, though at altitude where we were there was no noticeable change. At 2205, Basrah ATC called to say the weather was deteriorating, which started a few alarm bells ringing. We contacted the tasking authority to see if they were content for us to come off task, but they said 'No'. The RAF were still flying locally, which gave us some confidence, though we later discovered they were at low level and had a much better appreciation of the worsening conditions.

Descent back into Basrah was commenced at about 2240, ten mins ahead of the planned time. We still had good visual references on the ground and the RAF callsign was beginning his recovery. We descended to the west of the airfield, knowing it to be a clear area, but as we passed through 700 feet we could see that the picture outside bore no resemblance to that of only a few minutes earlier. The 'slant' visibility was extremely poor. As we had stacks of fuel left, I elected to go round for a GPS approach to give us time to settle down, having been at altitude for nearly 4 hours. As we were both relatively junior pilots, we didn't have too much experience of GPS let downs, though had carried out a couple each for practice previously.

The first approach was conducted by P2 in the right hand seat who flew it perfectly on the numbers, following the ideal track into the runway and passing the requisite heights at the correct distances. However, his approach was to a downwind runway, in recognition of the threat level rather than due to a sound Air Traffic Control requirement. When we got to 80 feet, the decision height, when the P2 stated he couldn't see anything and pulled power to overshoot.

In hindsight, I should have taken over then and landed, because I did have adequate visual references, but we also had plenty of fuel and there was no hurry. The aircraft was set up for a second approach, again to the downwind runway, but this turned out to be far worse, as neither of us could see a thing!

We climbed up to altitude again, and considered our

options. The whole of the Area of Operations around us appeared fogged out. The best airfield approach aid at Basrah was a Search Radar, which would only get us to around 200 feet - but we'd already been down to 80. There were no available diversions within fifty minutes flying time, which was our total fuel remaining. The only thing that seemed to be in our favour was that we did still have 30 minutes fuel above the minimum that we should land with. The tension was definitely rising; why on earth didn't we take notice of that first worsening weather call?

I flew the final approach, but elected to use the reciprocal runway and hence be into wind on final. I was to stay on instruments throughout, but the P2 would take control when and if he saw the ground. If he didn't, we'd simply land blind on the radar altimeter! Better this than land in the desert, because at least we knew the runway was flat and that the GPS would get us to it with accuracy. Largely because of the slower track across the ground and the fact that all the outside lighting sources were in front of us, we managed to land successfully in appalling visibility, P2 having seen the ground at the very last minute.

Having made it safely onto the runway, we couldn't then find the taxi-way and had to ask for a 'follow me' truck! The tower's last call was: *"If you lose the follow-me truck, just call us and we'll get him to slow down"*. I couldn't think of a smart answer to that, but was just mightily relieved to be there - and so pleased with the earlier decision to put another 600 lbs of fuel in...

LANDLOCKED IN A SEA OF SAND

Lt Dave Brewin   846 Sqn   2007

The dust, sand and mountains of Afghanistan have provided a dramatic backdrop for numerous wars over the millennia – involving the Persians, Mongols, Alexander the Great and in recent centuries, the British, the Soviets, Americans, the British (again!) as well as other NATO coalition forces. Now added to this list were the intrepid Naval aviators of the Commando Helicopter Force (CHF), who were adding their names in the history books of those that have done battle in this forbidding territory.

In January 2006, the rumours of a change of direction for 846 NAS operations became reality, when Colonel John McCardle RM, the Commander of CHF, confirmed that the Squadron would be deploying to Afghanistan in support of *Op Herrick*. As the first Royal Navy helicopters to be used in this theatre, 846 faced the considerable challenge of recovering to UK from its commitment in Iraq, and then upgrading its aircraft and their on-board equipment in less than seven months. For the pilots, of particular concern was the 'brown-out' effect of the dusty landing sites in Afghanistan. Fortunately, Junglies are well versed in this phenomenon, although more familiar with its brother, the 'white-out', in the snows of Norway, where pilots undergo their annual Arctic training.

Unlikely as it may seem, the months of preparation leading up to the deployment to Afghanistan began in the cold peaks and fjords around Bardufoss, 167 miles inside the Arctic Circle. The dust in Afghanistan is similar to very fine off-colour talcum powder, which envelops the whole of the aircraft in a cloud caused by the rotor downwash. This experience denies the pilot his normal visual references in the hover. The techniques learned for Norwegian landings in powder snow worked well in the demanding extremes of Afghanistan.

Following months of operational flying and infantry training, the squadron was put to the test during Exercise *Hida* (High Density Altitude) at RAF Akrotiri in Cyprus. The local areas provided both aircrew and ground-crew with a mountainous, dusty terrain. In September 2006, 3 *Sea King*s were transported by Antonov heavy-lift aircraft from RAF Brize Norton to RAF Akrotiri, Cyprus.

'Hot and high' is a phrase that most helicopter pilots understand well. The consequences of flying in these conditions cause the aircraft to under-perform, and the maximum AUW (All Up Weight) is markedly different from that pertaining at sea level. At altitude, the air is thinner and so more rotor blade pitch is required to provide an equivalent amount of lift to that required at sea level; there is an attendant increase in rotor 'drag.' Additionally, if the air is hotter the engine does not work nearly as well, reaching one of its limiting parameters earlier while trying to produce an equivalent amount of power. As a simple comparison, at *sea level* on a +15° C day, the maximum AUW is 21,400 lb; on another day, when at *10,000 feet* but at an air temp of +20°C, the maximum AUW falls to 16,500 lb, or some 2 tons *less*.

Fortunately, the recent *Sea King HC4+* upgrade has overcome these limitations, utilising Carson main rotor blades, a 5 bladed tail rotor, and certain improvements to the main rotor gearbox. The new Carson blades are a quantum leap in technology, having a differently-shaped aerofoil section, which twists along its length with a swept tip. The improvements in lift are quite marked, and it combats the onset of compressibility at higher forward speeds when at high altitude. An easily understood comparison is that the old rotor blade at 8000ft would only allow a forward airspeed of 80 knots, whereas the Carson blade pushed this up to 120 knots. It also gives a 2000 lb increase in load capacity at this altitude.

To fully capitalise on its merits, it had to be used in conjunction with the 'Indian' 5-blade tail-rotor. The original (1970) *Sea King* tail rotor had 5-blades, but during the Falklands War there were calls for greater performance, so Westlands gave it a 6-blade hub which *did* give better output, utilising two distinct rotor paths through an offset hub. However, there was a degree of blanking with this arrangement, and full design efficiency was never achieved.

All was not lost. Improved performance was derived by going back to a 5-blade setup, but with a reprofiled blade incorporating a bend at the root end, as developed years ago - and used by Indian Navy *Sea Kings*. Other new aircraft equipment included Display Night Vision Goggles (DNVG); 'Night Vision Goggles' are devices that amplify any incoming light by a factor of about 40,000. They first came into use with the RN in the 1970s and have proved to be extremely effective in numerous operational roles. Cockpits had to be heavily modified to dim all instrument and warning lighting to a level that was acceptable to the goggles. A 'normal' warning light amplified to this degree would cause temporary blindness and loss of night vision. Cockpits in the Fleet gradually became NVG compatible and pilots practised how to use them, especially at low level, to discover what could and could not be seen through them.

The world becomes somewhat mono-colour, in varying

shades of grey and green, but incredibly, most ground objects are readily visible providing there is some ambient light. For years, aviators also had to look back into the cockpit to study the various instrument readings; this was not an easy task when concentrating hard on the ground both ahead and around the aircraft. Now, the essential flight data was projected into the goggles, rather like a head-up display, ensuring that this form of flying is infinitely safer.

On 15 September 2007 Cdr Carretta, Commanding Officer 846 NAS, undertook the first flight of the newly upgraded Sea King HC4+, and later said: *"We are well used to working with the various elements of the Joint Helicopter Force, the difference now is that with the improved performance and capability of the up-rated Sea King HC4+ we can keep pace with other aircraft in theatre"*.

Cyprus provided suitable mountain flying training areas (Mount Olympus and The Troodos Mountains +30°C at 6,000ft) combined with a designated low flying training area. This proved to be ideal for undertaking dust and re-circulating sand landings and completing day and night operational sortie profiles. These included up to three ship helicopter tactical formations and other mission profiles. The detachment proved to be a resounding success for all and produced combat ready pilots for Afghanistan operations.

It was in the middle of a night in late November 2006 when personnel of D Flight, 846 Naval Air Squadron arrived in Afghanistan in a blacked-out RAF *TriStar*. Within just a few days the enhanced *Sea Kings* joined their maintainers and rapidly became embedded within the established *Lynx*, *Apache* and *Chinook* detachments of the Joint Helicopter Force (Afghanistan). Kandahar is home to some 15,000 military and civilian personnel from the US, Canada, Netherlands, Denmark, France and other nations. The barrack blocks of the base already seemed to make a pleasant change from the tents of Basra. Initially, flying was specifically focussed on familiarisation of the area by day and night, and becoming accustomed to the murk of dust landings while establishing the disposition of our own troops and trouble spots.

Operational flying commenced on 01 Dec 2007, when the *Sea Kings* assumed some of the operational burden by ensuring the flow of supplies across the scattered units in Helmand Province. Within a short period the remit of the *SK4+* expanded to include the whole of Regional Command South, covering an area greater than the size of Wales. Naturally, the 'lift and shift' capability of the aircraft was capitalised on, and the squadron were tasked with troop movements and under-slung loads throughout the entire region, with additional tasking such as mine-strike evacuation, command tasks and force protection. Force protection included the age-old technique of 'Eagle' Vehicle Check Points, where troops are dropped next to a road to check cars and vehicles for illegal weapons and explosives, with the *Sea King* then holding off as an aerial sentinel.

The advantage of this procedure is that once a vehicle or series of vehicles have been targeted, the occupants are unable to dispose of any incriminating items without being seen by either the troops on the ground or a sharp-eyed pilot or aircrewman. The aircraft would remain in radio contact with the troops, whilst maintaining a careful watch over a fairly wide area. A significant proportion of the squadron's tasking was working with aircraft from the coalition forces, in particular British or American *Apache* AH64 attack helicopters. These provided a heavily-armed escort to cover lifts into or out of known danger areas. During Forward Operations at Camp Bastion, the Sea Kings of the CHF were the High Readiness Force – held at short notice to carry out any of their essential roles during the assault by air on the Taliban stronghold of Musa Quala. As a result of this major attack in northern Helmand, the *Sea King* established itself as one of the major players in this theatre.

Camp life was bolstered in the run-up to Christmas when 846 NAS donned their Santa hats and the *Sea King* sleigh delivered up to 60 bags of Christmas mail and presents each day to the units scattered across the regional command. It was with a sigh of relief that the squadron was able to clear the entire backlog of free postal packages in time for the festive season. It was a massive undertaking as many parcels were addressed to troops in some of the most remote areas of Afghanistan, perched on outlying ridges and hidey holes.

The squadron also enjoyed some notable visitors over the festive season when *Top Gear* presenters Jeremy Clarkson, Richard Hammond and James May arrived in Kandahar. Many of our personnel had requested to grow beards whilst in Theatre, a not unusual pastime when away from home, but they rather wished they had not when the famous trio revelled in the opportunity to stand in for the Big Boss in a Detachment Commander's inspection, and displayed the kind of 'harsh banter' that many will have seen on their BBC television show. Another VIP visitor was the First Sea Lord, Admiral Sir Jonathon Band, who spent some time discussing challenging issues during a valuable 'question and answer' session. He had his ear bent a little, in traditional 'Jungly' fashion!

The winter months in Afghanistan have seen a determination on the part of the International Security Assistance Force to 'take the fight to the enemy', thus depriving the Taliban of their traditional rest and re-organisation periods in the mountains. The Naval *Sea Kings* are making a vital contribution to operations on the ground and have established an excellent reputation. The Jungly commitment to *Op Herrick* is now shared with 845 NAS, who arrived in Theatre in the spring of 2008. It is likely that Jungly personnel will spend three months in Afghanistan a year, with the rest of the time on other commitments, such as amphibious exercises and at home at their base at Yeovilton. Both 845 and 846 NAS have settled in well in Afghanistan. We find ourselves alongside our brother officers from the Naval Strike Wing with their *Harrier* GR7 and GR9's. So there is a strong Royal Navy presence in the mess and I guess you can go back to the section 'Junglies at play' to see what we get up to nowadays!

<u>847</u>

Lt Paul Whitehouse   **847 Sqn**   **2007**

The Commando Squadrons were always the main Royal Marines 'support' helicopter element, but in addition there was a lighter squadron, owned and operated by the Royal Marines themselves. Initially this started out using '*M*A*S*H*' type Bell 47 *Sioux* helicopters, piston-engined, and capable of carrying one or sometimes two passengers or a stretcher. This outfit was known as 3 Cdo Brigade Air Squadron (3 BAS) and was an integral part of the Commando Brigade, each individual Commando unit having its own flight. 3 BAS subsequently re-equipped with Army versions of the *Scout* and then *Gazelle* and *Lynx*.

However, finance and politics dictated a change, and in 1995 3 BAS was re-aligned with the Royal Navy's Commando Squadrons, as 847. Of the 21 pilots on strength at present only 6 are Royal Marines the remainder being Royal Navy. However, more RMs are now flying the *Sea King 4* and even the *Chinook,* and at least three (as of 2008) have qualified on the ground-attack *Harrier.* The maintenance staff are now mostly Royal Navy, having taken over from the REME engineers of 3 BAS in 2003.

I passed along what is now a well-established path for a Naval Aviator, through Joint Flying Training: Dartmouth 'officer school'; grading flights on the *Grob*; Slingsby *Firefly* fixed-wing training at Barkston Heath, and then helicopters at RAF Shawbury. I was one of four Naval pilots on a course learning to fly the AS350 *Squirrel*, the other eight being Army and RAF. I soon got used to the delightful aeroplane - and somehow managed to bluff my way through the course, at the end of which we were selected for the next stage of training. Our knowledge base was a little thin, but we had listened to the 'dits' our instructors spun and decided in our own minds which way we wanted to go.

There was also the question of where we were needed and who had 'vacancies', which would be a major factor in our selection. The choices were Jungly *Sea King 4*, '*Grey Lynx*' on the back of a small ship, *Merlin* anti-submarine and sometimes *Sea King SAR*, but not the latter two for my course. I had decided some time before that the Jungly ethos was the only way for me - and pressed for it as strongly as I was able. The day came and I was invited into the CO's office - to be told that I would undertake 'OTP'. *"OTP, sir? Where does that come between Shawbury and the 848 Jungly Sea King conversion course?"* It was then I learnt that I was bound for 670 Sqn of the Army Air Corps at Middle Wallop and - ultimately - 847 NAS!

I arrived at Middle Wallop with a little trepidation, nervously looking around at people stamping about in shiny boots, and with creases in their shirtsleeves you could shave with. I tried to iron some formal creases into my fresh-out-of-the-bag green fatigues and add some black polish to my boots, but it didn't seem to make much difference. When I met the rest of the course in Stockwell Hall, I realised I would have to fall back on the age old defensive routines: "*I'm a matelot! Can you show me how to turn this iron on again?*" They all seemed nice normal people though, as well as easily approachable - except for the big Para, who looked as if he ate small children for dinner!

So I relaxed a little, and things were moving along nicely, I seemed to be on the course register, in the right place and at the right time - good start! Then Mr Pendrey, the A Flight Commander turned to me and asked in no uncertain terms: "*Navy chappie, why on earth are you here?*" A stunned silence in the briefing room followed. I timidly answered: "*I am hoping to go to 847 sir, if I pass the course.*"

"*Ah, well you won't do too badly going there...*" he muttered, with just the hint of a smile. It was after this, when listening to tales about the ships he had been on, (whilst I was barely a twinkle in my parents' eyes), I learnt about the illustrious 3 BAS, the precursor to 847 Squadron. The following weeks on Ground School helped me to settle in to the normal student pattern again. Learn, perfom, learn and perform again etc. I had to translate a few times to my course colleagues what his use of the terms *Cabin, Wet, Scran, Oggin and Teeny Weeny* actually meant, but on the whole I was feeling comfortable. The culmination of the intense ground school period was an Air Observation Post (AOP) shoot with a staff pilot flying, me in the front and an 'expert' in the back. Please remember this is the first time I have seen anything bigger than a firework Roman Candle go off - and I was certainly a little excited!

It was a cold day out in the middle of Salisbury plain, especialy up in the helicopter, and the staff artillery officer in the rear could not get his headset to work. Here I was, with twenty-five Point Detonating artillery rounds ready to let loose - and the helicopter's communication systems were playing up! Frustration was building up and it was five minutes in the hover before we managed to 'cuff' something together. My first shoot, '*Targeting for future engagement*' went well, so we moved swiftly to the second, which was straight '*Target destruction*'. It took me five rounds to bracket the target, getting ever closer by adjusting the fall of shot up or down, leaving me with four rounds '*Fire for effect*', in salvoes of three. That meant 12 rounds in one quick firing burst.

The litany of: "*Fire over, Fire out*" "*Splash over, splash out*" rang through the headset to advise of the progress being made. The target disappeared in cordite smoke and soil with small *'grumphs'* clearly heard in the aircraft three kilometres away. The target could not possibly survive my barrage and I was very pleased indeed. The quick debrief didn't mention my destructive prowess, but seemed to concentrate on how many *"overs"*, *"outs"* and *"this is"* I had missed, using the unfamiliar Army radio voice procedure, but I nonetheless left with a huge smile. Job done!

The following two months saw me continue on 'A' flight, the handling part of 670 Sqn, without much mishap, before moving on. One major difference between 670 and RAF Shawbury was single pilot operations. Shawbury had just changed from teaching single pilot navigation, because all RAF helicopters are now twin crew, and only the Navy and Army fly single pilot ops. This latter skill was taught on Nav 1 and we were expected to be competent by the second sortie, Nav 2! The major problem with single pilot navigation is cockpit management, particularly what to do with a map the size of a blanket. Some instructors would take control whilst you refolded the map, to simulate landing on and performing the task on the ground. Other instructors just said: *"Cope!"* Once I asked if I could hold the stick with my teeth whilst at low level to enable me to map fold. I was feeling a little sorry for myself at the time. Again all I heard was *"Cope!"* You quickly learned to fold your map to be able to get to any part of it easily, using only one hand.

My main instructor on 'A' flight was Nigel North, an ex Jungly pilot from Yeovilton. He was an excellent teacher and, I later learned, a well-decorated legend within the Commando world, having done a good deal of the night insertions of Special Forces in the Falklands, often in appalling weather. The key to a good grade from Nige, I quickly learnt, was to make sure he was well fed. On a landaway to the South West I planned Dartmouth Naval College as the first stop - and lunch in the Wardroom. With Nige humming happily to himself after a good feast, it was always going to be a good sortie! Our time on 'A' flight concentrated on flying the aircraft, general handling, instrument flying, formation and all that sort of thing.

The start of 'B' flight was again two weeks of ground school. Here we were taught intermediate tactics, building on what we had leaned at Sandhurst or in NCO cadres. *"Erm, excuse me, I'm Navy and haven't done any of that"*, I would warble. *"You do tactics at Dartmouth don't you?"* I was asked. *"We once went out on Dartmoor and bivvied"*, I replied with complete honesty. *"Ahem - yes, well if you have any questions stay behind and we will try and explain it to you"*.

The culmination of tactics ground school was 4 days in the ACTT, (Aviation Command Tactics Trainer) which if it wasn't so serious, seemed like a giant computer game. Each sortie was preceded by a set of 'orders', which are a pre-ordained method of passing on the battle plan to all of your own troops, in 'Army speak' of course. The tactical Flight Reference Cards (FRCs) had comprehensive templates for aviation orders, so with a few examples and helpful tips and hints from course mates I managed to get through the process. One issue I did have was with the acronyms used for the various regiments. I felt fairly justified at this confusion:

"Who's 1 WFR?"
"Oh, they're the Worcestershire and Sherwood Foresters."
"RGJ?"
"Royal Green Jackets"
"PWRR?"
"Prince of Wales Royal Regiment"
"PARA?"
"Don't be daft - The Parachute Regiment"

I should have known that - one of them was a course mate!

After ground school, our group went to RAF Henlow for the Night Vision Goggles course, which proved to be an excellent afternoon's instruction expanded into two days. A lot of discussion took place in the main bar! My main memory of 'B' flight was the banter. It was endless in the crewroom, and may I now publicly apologise to anybody who received applications for the Army Bell-ringing Society, or to join the Ronald McDonald club. The course's biggest boy, our Para, did get a large proportion of the banter. He regularly received photos of old people in aircraft, sheep and First World War aircraft in the mail system, especially from the course NCOs. Each was proudly placed next to the other above his desk.

My lasting memory of the banter though, will be of the day when one of the braver NCOs rang the crewroom phone from his mobile across the room:

"670 Squadron, B flight students' crewroom, Captain PARA

speaking".

"HELLLLOOOOO!" came the reply, in a slightly high pitched, Scottish and definitely feminine voice. Our Para sniffed loudly once, immediately sensing the ruse, calmly put the phone down, slowly bent below his desk and unbeknown to everybody unplugged the phone. He then rose in an explosion of movement that had to be seen to be appreciated - and launched the phone across the room, missing the NCOs head by an inch and gouging a chunk out of the wall behind. That particular jape was never repeated - and the phone never worked again.

The flying conducted on 'B' flight is easily some of the best you do in the flying training system; tactical low flying, night flying and NVG low flying at night being the most demanding. If you have a good imagination, you can really get into the hordes of enemy forces sweeping north across Devon, as you engage them with artillery and send position reports back on recce missions during Exercise *Woodlark*. My lasting memory of *Woodlark* will be Peter, last seen protruding from my *Squirrel* helicopter. Peter was the large herring gull that took this bigger 'bird' head on and lost, but putting a foot square hole in the nose of the aircraft, whilst we were at low level south of Barnstaple. The resulting 'bang', feathers floating in the cockpit and smell of burnt bird guts made the instructor land in a field and be sick - and I thought the Army chaps were made of sterner stuff!

The culmination of our flying course was the Final Handling Test, a sortie we dreaded, not knowing what was likely to be thrown at us. I flew mine with the Chief Flying Instructor who had a bit of a reputation for accuracy and logic. How do you swat up for that? The sortie went OK until I arrived back at the base, hovering over the spot and with only thirty seconds left of the trip. This aircraft simply would not land! After the prescribed thirty seconds, with the hover monkeys hanging off the skids and affecting the balance of my aircraft, I decided, wrongly probably, to get the aircraft on the deck. So with teeth gritted, I lowered the collective and put the skids on in a reasonably firm fashion. Only nerves of course!

At this point the CFI turned to me and said, *"Reverting to type are we? Nice deck landing!"* Oh well, a kill is a kill, however it is achieved. I did pass, and was very proud to wear my Naval wings

163

- a trained pilot at last.

The next move in the pipeline was to 671 Sqn, where I met the *Lynx AH7*. As ever the ground school came first, frustratingly keeping us away from the aeroplane, but also the simulator got in the way of flying. Simulators are cheaper and easier to keep going than the real thing and have the added advantage that any number of problems can be injected into a sortie, something you can't always do for real. We did ultimately get to the aeroplane - and what a difference it was, and how good it felt to fly. The course lasted 36 flying hours, but also included 45 simulator hours. The White instrument rating is gained in the simulator. Flying a front line twin -engined helicopter was a huge leap in technology to take, but that feeling of confidence and pride cannot be overstated. It felt very good indeed.

The end of 671 Sqn was almost 4 years to the day since I had commenced my training at Dartmouth - from September 2003 to October 2007. Well, here I was at last, fully trained and ready for the front line. I finished 671 on Friday, officially joined 847 the following Monday, but then found that I had been on my new squadron's night flying programme the Wednesday before! Never mind though, the reasons were very valid; the team was under-borne by 4 pilots, or nearly 20%. Sadly, as often happens in the Navy, the tasking just kept piling in.

The next rude shock was that before Christmas, I deployed to Basrah airbase in Iraq, where life was quite different. The flying was excellent, including some Special Forces Ops that drum up images of cloak-and-dagger stuff, but of course I can't go into that element of our operations, or I'd be arrested and thrown into the Tower of London. Day-to-day tasking was light utility and surveillance. The *Lynx* is a small helicopter; in the hot and high desert it can only carry four passengers. We were therefore used for only small moves, while carrying small amounts of kit. With the strategic move of troops out of Basrah city to the airport, there were fewer personnel moves to do. The *Lynx Mk 9* used in Basrah also has a camera on the side which was used to observe and record the goings on in various parts of the city, as when supporting convoy moves from the south. Operating over a convoy in the middle of the night, flying high level circles round the slow-moving trucks could be a little painful.

The social side of Basrah was seriously unimpressive. My first notion was that a desert would be baking hot and dry, but in the winter this one was cold, wet and muddy most of the time! Most things were best done from the safe side of a blast wall; even the Portakabins we lived in were protected by blast walls. Inside each Portakabin was the 'coffin', which was a bunker built around your mattress with a small hole to squeeze in and out of, obviously to protect you from explosive blast. It was actually quite nice once you got used to it, but was as effective at trapping the cold as it was in protecting you and it was very cold over Christmas.

At the air station there were daily rocket attacks, which restricted us moving around the base easily. I did not give much thought to the loud bangs when I first arrived, it being my first time in theatre. However, I was in my 'coffin' one day when the rocket alarm went off (and I still twitch now when I hear a similar car alarm), I had just turned over in bed and was trying to get back to sleep when an almighty bang went off. It wasn't just heard; it was physically and quite strongly felt. You know an explosion is close when you feel it both in the air and *through* the ground. As I hunched into the foetal position I heard lumps of soil, gravel and sand rattling on the roof of my Portakabin. After that, I was an awful lot quicker into cover every time I heard the alarm. I also hit the ground in London, during the first weekend back with my girlfriend, when a car alarm went off.

The downtime activities were a little limited and certainly bore no resemblance to 'standard' military off-time habits of frequenting the local bars. There was a gym. On Saturday night we were allowed two cans of beer, but otherwise the base was dry. Even then we struggled to get to the bar on Saturdays due to our crew duty notice hours. You could not drink alcohol ten hours before you flew; if on the program, you were at 60 minutes notice to move. I was duty on Christmas day and did not have a drink then, which was the first dry Crimbo I have had since Santa first called to bring my presents. So with the very small range of distractions available, I became a fan of various television series. Most people on the squadron had a couple of personal DVDs, and these were regularly swapped. It is amazing how many episodes of '24' and 'Prison Break' you could watch in an off day!

With the introduction into service of the *Apache* in 2005,

Lynx 7s and *9s* had their missile systems removed, which was a shame - and gave us a slightly more restricted role. We are however, very much in demand and the Jungly ethos of 'get the job done' is still very much behind our mission tasking. Being back with the Navy is excellent after such a long time in a 'purple' (Army/Navy/Air Force) training environment. For a multi-role squadron, there is always masses to do. The Junglies answer to two taskmasters, C-in-C 'Land' through the Joint Helicopter Command, and C-in-C 'Fleet' for the preservation of the UK's 'littoral manoeuvre' (amphibious) capability.

Therefore, whenever we are on downtime between operations in Afghanistan and Iraq, we must do our best to stay proficient in embarked operations. At present, the squadron is training for a six month deployment to Afghanistan starting in October 2008, but also looking further forward to an amphibious deployment to the Far East, shortly after our return.

THE GREEN HOLE

Lt J J Hughes   **845 Sqn**   **2003**

Operation TELIC began for me with a very, very long three months deployment. There were times of utter madness matched almost equally by periods of total boredom, all of which had to be approached in their own special way to ensure personal survival in the blue and orangey brown landscape of the Arabian Gulf. Through all the varied situations I encountered, there was one night that stood out in particular - 4 hours and 50 minutes flying to be exact. This will be my lasting memory of being a part of 845 Naval Air Squadron during war Operations in Southern Iraq.

On Thursday, 20 March 2003, the day started with me dragging myself from a rather comfortable American cot bed situated within '*The Green Hole*' of Camp Viking at around 0730 Central, or 0430Z (Greenwich Mean Time) which we were all supposed to be using, because units from various geographic locations needed a consistent time base to work from. The day, or the forenoon at least, was supposed to be one for obtaining much-deserved rest - because that night was just possibly going to be ***the*** night! The night for what? The night that the war against Iraq would officially start, and the night that nine *Sea King 4* crews from the mighty Eight Hundred and Forty Fifth would insert elements of 40 Commando Royal Marines into the Al Faw Peninsula – the southern-most tip of Iraq.

We didn't know at this early point in the day exactly what we would experience later on, because the decision to 'go in' could have been 'yesterday' and it could just as likely be 'tomorrow', so no one was really holding their breath at this stage that later on they might be flying the most demanding sorties of their lives.

The next 12 hours formed its own pattern – we'd be having a brief, or a meeting, eating lunch, perhaps taking a worried 'hope this'll be over ever so quick' type moment, or even just sitting about chewing the fat, when suddenly Landrover horns would sound and we'd all dive into the nearest shell-scrape to get some protection. The horns meant a possible *Scud* missile/chemical attack inbound and I think they sounded about seventeen times that day. So of course the *last* thing we had was a really relaxing day before the night's exertions, because of worries that a missile might land on our heads at any moment.

We thought the 'insert' would take place tomorrow since this was what we had been led to believe by the powers that be. But at about 1500hrs Central Time the news came in that it would in fact be *tonight*! This wasn't a big problem since the majority of the briefs and planning were already complete, so all that was required was one last confirmation of all the details, stretched out by constant interruption of the Landrover horns, of course.

All that was required now was for all the right-hand seat pilots (of which I was one – can't believe it took me so long to mention this most essential point for what comes later in the story), to go out to the aircraft and turn them all around through 180 degrees because over the course of the day the wind had reversed in direction. Turning nine aircraft and arranging a total swap around of positions was not the easiest process when moving one at a time, but eventually, by 1830C, I sat down to rest for what felt like the first time during the day.

H-Hour (the nominated time that everything was set to kick off) was to be 1900Z, or 2200C. It can get quite complicated working domestically in one time zone and operationally to

167

another, 3 hours earlier. My crew was due to lift at approximately H + 1hr 45mins, we were callsign *Whiskey Nine*, crew *India* and the plan for the evening looked like this:

1)   From H-Hour, be on call to lift at approx H + 1.45.

2)   Launch as number four in a formation with underslung mortars to be dropped off at an oil pipeline feed out to the ocean named 'LS Maple'.

3)   Return to *The Green Hole* for hot refuel, then latch on as number six in a formation with underslung bergens to be dropped at the Main Oil Metering Station named LS Dogwood.

4)   Pick up nets at LS Dogwood after dropping bergens and take them back to HMS *Ocean* to remain on call for further tasking.

The actual course of events ran a little differently, and it is worth mentioning at this juncture that at no point in the lead up to the mission did we have a proper run-through or rehearsal. Two rehearsals did in fact take place, one at night (the very delayed day rehearsal, in which I didn't fly because at this early planning stage I was not to be part of the 'first wave') and one in the early hours of the actual day (the much delayed 'night' rehearsal) and for neither of these was a single load rigged or flown. In hindsight, as you will see from the next few paragraphs, this would probably have proved quite helpful! So at about H + 30, we in crew *India* manned up our *Sea King 4* and the following five hours will stay with me forever as my lasting memory of the 'first wave into Al Faw':

It was very noticeable, as soon we were in the aircraft, that the weather did not look the best. One of the main reasons that tonight had been chosen for the insert was that there was quite a good moon, meaning that flying with our Night Vision Goggles (NVGs) should be made easier. But as I started up the cab, put my NVGs down over my eyes and adjusted their focus, it was apparent that the visibility had closed in quite a lot from earlier in the day.

The goggles give an eerie green glow to everything, but you can see immeasurably more than with the naked eye. I wasn't overly concerned though, because there was a large amount of helicopter movement around the area. At H-Hour RAF *Chinook* and USMC *MH53* helicopters had started arriving and departing from the area of *The Green Hole*, meaning that an awful lot of dust had already been stirred up. It was therefore only natural to assume that the apparent loss in visibility was down all the extra dust being blown around, and this would only be a localised effect at *The Green Hole*.   My growing suspicions that everything might not be quite right began when the first *Sea King* (*Whiskey 5* if my memory serves me correctly) lifted from the fuelling point within *The Green Hole*, did more than one circuit, overshot each approach to land and eventually landed about a quarter of a mile further south. We wondered what the hell they were up to and it wasn't until later that I learned that *Whiskey 5* had to land next to the illuminated landing aid of the NATO 'T' to our south - because he could see nothing else!

I lifted into the hover using a black oil barrel as my reference marker, but this soon disappeared into a cloud of dust, so outside the window there were now no visual cues at all - I reverted immediately to instrument flying, knowing that within a couple of seconds we would rise clear of the dust cloud. However, within *The Green Hole* what was normal didn't necessarily apply, for when I looked up from the instruments at about 100 feet I still couldn't make out any features, and there was absolutely *no* horizon.

If I'm brutally honest I have to say this was a massive surprise, and it scared me stupid. It's difficult to describe the conditions, but can you imagine a never-ending supply of brown talcum powder being whipped up in a huge cloud when acted upon by an oversized fan? In snow, the particles are more dense and generally heavier, so climbing out of clag is very much easier. This talcum powder was aided and abbetted by *fog* on which the solid dust particles settled, blanking out any view. The terrain was a natural 'cold soak' area - where cool air moved downhill into the bowl in which we were now trapped.

I looked back inside at the instruments and saw the nose was high, speed low, wings not level, though thankfully we were still climbing through 200ft - but things were all starting to look very wrong. I had to concentrate hard at this point, putting all my training into practice to get the aircraft back into a safe flight configuration! I focussed on the instruments and by sheer will power got us back down to 100ft, at about 60kts and stable, now in the circuit and trying to avoid all the other aircraft we could hear on the radio in the area.

Looking down at where we had taken off from, we tried to sight our re-fuelling point, but where the hell was it? The visibility was really bad and the features on the ground so difficult to make out that it was extremely difficult to find our area. Eventually I heard, *'got it, left at 8 o'clock'* from my co-pilot, followed by *'turn now and you'll be set up nicely to land.'* So I turned left, and sure enough there was something on the nose within the murk, so I made my approach. But something still definitely wasn't right. We came down through 80 feet, 70, 60, 50, 40 - and still I couldn't make out the ground properly, as there was absolutely no contrast whatsoever - 30, 20 and I was still not happy with the visual references.

"Overshooting!" I called, and began climbing away from our landing area into the Big Green once more, although this time I was a bit more prepared, and kept a much better scan on the instruments. It was now clear why *Whiskey 5* had overshot their first approach, because it was going to be bloody hard to land within *The Green Hole*. Downwind in the 'circuit' we chatted to each other as a crew and calmed ourselves down a bit, all three of us expressing that this was a complete nightmare!

I spotted the re-fuelling area earlier this time around and set myself up better for the approach, taking it very slowly and deliberately. 80 feet, 70, 60, 50, 40 - still no references - 30, 20, 15 - *'Happy with my references'* I eventually called to the crew, though I have to say 'unhappy and barely adequate' would have described my feelings rather better! A heavy and wobbly landing followed, but we were back on the ground and plugged in for a top-up of fuel.

At this point I must have let out a huge sigh of relief; I don't think that I have ever had to work so hard to get a helicopter back on the ground, in fact I know that I haven't. I was scared and did not want to have to get airborne again in that weather, in this area - although this is what my job was all about, I was going to have to work harder tonight just to stay alive in friendly territory than I have ever done before, and at this point we hadn't even crossed over enemy lines into Iraq!

The fuel came in way too quick for my liking, and it was soon time to take off again. If someone had come over the radio right then and said *'All Whiskey callsigns, cancel and shutdown where you are'* I would have done so, no questions asked - indeed I was wishing for that to happen. It didn't, and as we launched again into *The Green Hole* to reposition, the same pattern of events happened – the oil barrel I had used earlier that day as a landing reference was now next to useless – so we overshot and once more I was all nerves, forcibly calming myself down for the next attempt. The ground was still not visible until somewhere between 15 and 5 feet but I managed to get us safely down on the ground again.

Dear God, how many times am I going to have to do this? I was counting through in my head, wishing for time to speed up, accelerate so that it was daylight, then morning and everything would be over - but, no, not yet - the call came over the radio that it was time for us to pick up our loads and head off into Iraq.

I don't think I shall ever forget that load - mortars for 40 Commando. It was the biggest net of stuff that I have ever had to lift, supposedly weighing 3500lbs, which was not a heavy load by *Sea King* standards, but as we were full of fuel as well, it made the whole deal very heavy indeed. I also suspect that the declared weight was a little bit of an under-estimation, a not unusual situation when taking 'Royal' into battle.

The first problem with the load was always going to be picking it up; by the time that the hover reference turned up (a LandRover positioned out in my one o'clock by about 20 metres) the first two aircraft in our formation of four had departed, so we were now a formation of two, *Whiskeys 8* and *9*. Right then - I took another deep breath, *'Ready to lift...'* I took off into the hover and all I could see was that LandRover; everything else was dust.

I fixed my attention on that single point as the only way of telling my position, but this load was going to be a real pig – '*Left 2 yards, forward 3 yards, left 1 yard, right 4 yards, back 2 yards*' called the crewman, but it was so hard to make these small adjustments having only the single point of reference!

Eventually, after what seemed like a lifetime, we hooked on. '*Clear above, clear to lift*' said the crewman, and I pulled in power to commence the climb and immediately lost the LandRover. Back on instruments again, '*Keep pulling in power, keep lifting...*' I heard from the crewman, who was looking vertically down and could still make out the Landrover, which wasn't getting any smaller.

The cab wasn't going up, so I increased power, 110%, 115%,

120% torque, then we started to go up, but very slowly. The collective was high, too high, all I had were my instruments in that dust cloud and I didn't like what I saw – the radar altimeter tells you how close you are to the ground, and the rate of climb or descent indicator (RCDI) tells you if you're going up or down; it's always nice when taking off to look at these two dials and see them both going up. But they weren't!

That dust cloud lasted for an eternity – 30 feet, 40, 30 again - 40 - 35 - 40 - 45 – we were really struggling to go up. *'Increase your speed'* muttered the co-pilot, so I gingerly put the nose forward, 20 knots, 30 - 40, and then along with the speed increase came transational lift, then a climb and we were slowly, ever so slowly, edging ourselves away from the ground, with the load gently swinging away under the cab. We had our load and we were heading into Iraq with *Whiskey 8,* at 50kts because the load wouldn't allow us to fly any faster! It proved necessary to instrument fly the 30 miles or so into Iraq, at 100 feet-ish, with a heavy underslung load at 50 knots and nothing visible outside the window; we were navigating on GPS alone. This was not what I had imagined war was going to be like, but was quite clearly the way it was going to be for now.

So, the transit passed slowly but quite calmly, and here we were about to cross the border for the first time. With all our checks complete, and all of the new and improved Defensive Aids Suite turned on - in case anyone fired something at us our chances of survival were very much enhanced. But no one did fire anything, and even as we approached the site to drop off the load you could actually see the ground! For the first time in this already far too emotional night I could see…things and *stuff*!

We came into the hover and dropped the load – easily. Then we did a really punchy departure, because we we were as hard as nails! I now loved Iraq – nobody shot at me and I can see the ground, I'm out of *The Green Hole*, this place is great, I can't wait to come back. However, we were heading back into that dreaded location to pick up more fuel - and our next load.

The re-fuel wasn't as bad the second time around but something struck me when we arrived shakily back on the ground – I wasn't the only one out here having a hard time, others were finding it difficult too.

We took our fuel, plus a little extra to make it to the ship after our drop, then repositioned to the left of the underslung bergens we were going to have to lift next. After the emotionally draining experience of the 40 Commando mortars, these bergens I soon discovered were my new best friends – I had more than one reference point when in the hover, a second LandRover with a further netful of bergens re-assuringly close.

The pick-up this time was like taking sweets from a baby - and considerably lighter! We launched for the second time on our way towards Iraq and, as we now knew, an escape from *The Green Hole*. But things never seem to go quite as smoothly as they should. Once we exited *The Green Hole* and crossed the border once more, we were held off to the south of LS Dogwood by about a mile - because they were taking fire! This was a new dimension, and now I was uncomfortable again – I could see the ground, but I was uneasy for a different reason – here we were in a big old *Sea King* at about 100ft, driving ourselves around in circles, with an underslung load, at or around 60kts and only a few hundred metres away from the shooting! I was *not* happy...

'This isn't right guys, I don't like this hanging around in enemy territory stuff one bit...' but eventually after five minutes or so we got the all clear to go into the LS.

A better or quicker load drop off have I ever done? Not likely, I was awesome, so awesome in fact and so keen to head off back to the ship that I forgot all about the nets we were supposed to pick up. The crewman bless him, reminded us just as we were starting to accelerate back towards safety. A quick turn around and we landed, but where were the nets? Behind us – so we lifted, did a spot turn, quickly hover taxied the 100m or so behind us, spot turn back into wind and landed with the nets right next to the cargo door – I was pretty damn good at this NVG flying malarkey now that I could see the ground! We got the nets on board and this time were away back to normality, with another massive sigh of relief, it was nearly all over.

But there was one last little bit of excitement for us that night. About 20 seconds after an extremely racy departure from Dogwood we were nearly hit by something. I don't really know what it was, probably a mortar bomb, but it exploded very close to our aeroplane, and I felt the explosion shake the aircraft and the heat of whatever it was enveloped me. I was seriously alarmed and my heart really started pumping...

This was the fitting end that I could really have done without; I accelerated, went off heading, very nearly flew TOO low, but then regained my senses - we weren't being fired at anymore, if indeed they had been firing at us in the first place. The journey home to Mother took about half an hour I think, but all that I really remember was *Ocean* appearing out of the murk and what a beautiful sight she was! Never had I been so pleased to view her awkward, chubby-looking outline.   We landed on and were suddenly safe; the relief was immense – another crew were coming out to swap with us, and we could go inside for some much needed sleep. Which after around half a pack of cigarettes I duly did!

The above is the story of my personal and lasting memory of the first day of that war, something I shall never forget and also never regret, because I was there, and will forever be one of the old boys of 845!

A JUNGLY SECRET REVEALED

GOODBYE, OLD FRIEND

Lt Richard Hutchings RM   **846 SqnMay 1982**

Night Vision Goggles (NVG) were relatively new in 1982 and their effectiveness was not generally appreciated. However, a small flight of three aircraft of 846 Sqn carried out Special Forces operations at night, extremely successfully, including the destruction of twelve ground attack aircraft at Pebble Island airfield. In the following excerpt from his excellent book 'Special Forces Pilot', Dick Hutchings tells of the end of a one way mission to drop SAS troops on mainland Argentina to raid the base believed to house Super Etendard aircraft which were a formidable threat to the task force. After a maximum range six hour flight at very low level, having not been able to land at the correct site because of fog, the SAS were dropped on the Argentine/Chilean border and Dick and his crew flew on to Punta Arenas and destroyed the aircraft to disguise the nature of their mission.

Although we had made many holes with an axe in the helicopter's fuselage, a flat calm sea condition had not been anticipated. I left Wiggy and Pete on the beach and flew the aircraft on my own to purposely ditch it at sea, just off the coast. However, with a boat-shaped hull to facilitate water landings, it remained stubbornly upright and stable on the surface, with no hint of it rocking from side to side or sinking of its own accord. I could have waited longer, but decided that the best course of action was to fly back to the beach and make more and larger holes in the bottom of the fuselage. The last-words to me from the Captain of HMS *Hermes* had been loud and clear: "*Having dropped the SAS off, take no unnecessary risks and don't do anything foolhardy...*" I reasoned that what I was now attempting to do was both a necessary and calculated risk to ensure operational secrecy and was not unduly foolhardy - but that is for others to judge!

While flying back to the beach, the fuel low level warning lights now came on constantly, indicating that the fuel level was (in normal circumstances) dangerously low. This wasn't really an issue - given that I was about to destroy the aircraft and there were still a few minutes of fuel remaining. However, much more to the point was that I was now blinded, not intermittently, but *permanently* by the massive magnification of these wretched warnings provided by my high-tech goggles. The circuit breakers to douse them were inaccessible to me on my own, high up on the panel - and both my hands were full with flying the helicopter. Unable to see where I was going, I carried on slowly towards the beach as best I could.

My arrival there was unexpected and as I attempted to manoeuvre the aircraft to line up with the length of the beach, I saw the shadowy figures of Wiggy and Pete running for cover behind the sand dunes. I was now without any real external visual references, and quite unable to correct any sideways movement of the airframe, because I didn't know it was moving that way! Eventually the aircraft made a very hard landing on the sloping beach, resulting in the port undercarriage collapsing and the main rotor blades making contact with the sand dunes to my left. With the helicopter about to shake itself to pieces, I closed the fuel cut-off levers - which had the effect of stopping both engines. I quickly applied the rotor brake and with the *Sea King* now perched precariously on its left side, climbed out in a most unaccustomed way - uphill. As I stood on the beach surveying the wreckage, I glanced at my watch; it was a little after 0615 and it would be dawn in another hour. We had much to do and not much time in which to do it.

I considered it essential to burn the seriously damaged *Sea King* to destroy any clues as to the nature of our mission and not compromise the troops we had left. In amongst our kit there were two gallons of petrol as fuel for our small cooker, and I also had the two explosive devices given to me by Captain A of the SAS an hour earlier.

Before setting fire to the aircraft, Wiggy and I destroyed the NVG as we had been ordered - so as not to leave any hint of our operating methods. The goggles were smashed into small pieces using boulders on the beach and the pieces thrown into the sea. It did cross my mind that our vandalism was costing about £20,000 a set of NVG and the aircraft about £4,000,000! With all of our kit placed behind the dunes, I re-entered the *Sea King* and turned the battery master switch on so that I could drain what little engine fuel remained in the tanks to form a small pool under the aircraft. I next poured one gallon of the petrol over the inside of the aircraft from the cockpit to the main door - and threw into the cabin the two explosive devices set for delayed detonation. Finally, I ignited and then threw a night distress flare into the aircraft cabin, as well as the second flare underneath the aircraft, into the puddle of fuel.

In a flash the helicopter was burning fiercely; within one minute much of the main cabin had been consumed by fire and the main rotor gearbox had collapsed from its carefully engineered position and settled onto the ground. After two minutes the charges exploded. With the aircraft well ablaze, Wiggy, Pete and I then grabbed our bergens, crossed the minor road and made our way up into the hills to the west.

Where it all began - an American built S-55 Whirlwind HAR.21, fitted with Pratt & Whitney engine, providing an immense leap in mobility for the ground troops operating in the Malayan jungle during the 1950s where they made itup as they went along, and from whence the name 'Jungly' derived.

The British-built Westland Whirlwind HAS.7, with Alvis Leonides engine, having trouble with an underslung load on the flight deck of HMS *Bulwark*.

Wessex HAS.1 XP112 ('G') lies ruined at Sibu, Sarawak, after entering ground resonance and colliding with XP155 ('B'), 13 June 1964.

Troops go through the ritual of assembling and emplaning in Wessex prior to being ferried ashore. Late 1960s in HMS *Bulwark*.

A broken Sioux AH.1 of 3 Commando Brigade Air Squadron is underslung
to RNAS Sembawang, Singapore, by a Wessex HU.5 of 847 Sqn, 1970.

A Wessex HU.5 of 847 Sqn troop dropping in Brunei during exercise 'New look II', May 1971.

Having absorbed the five Wessex of 847 Sqn, the 'back to normal' twenty one Wessex HU.5s of 848 Sqn disembark to Simbang in May 1971 (one u/s aircraft still in *Albion*).

HMS *Albion* en-route to provide flood relief in Pakistan during November 1971 with twenty two Wessex HU.5s of 848 Sqn and two Sea King HAS.1s of 826 Sqn embarked. Note the Union flag on the flight deck.

Sea King HC.4 cross decking stores as underslung loads, SS *Canberra* in the background, Falklands Conflict, 1982.

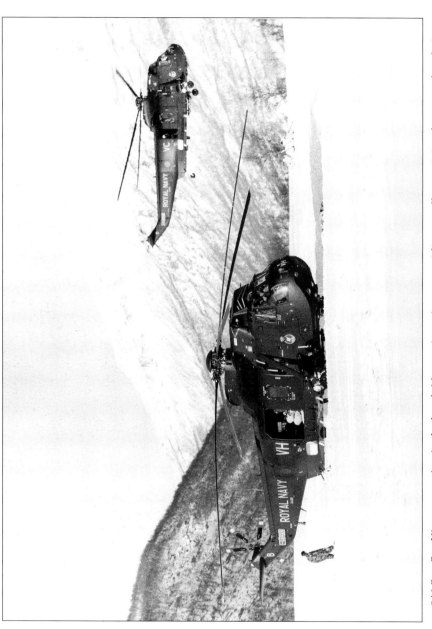

846 Sqn Sea Kings operating in the harsh Norwegian winter, providing excellent training for ground and air crews alike.

Arctic camouflaged Sea King HC.4, streaked with tell tale hydraulic fluid, hooking on a load at RNoAF Bardufoss in 1988. Not all aircraft were thus marked as the green standard scheme also works well.

'Jungly' Sea King HC.4s on United Nations peacekeeping duties in the very distinctive white colour scheme in Bosnia, 1993.

A Sea King HC.4 of 845 Sqn landing civilian refugees during the Bosnian conflict, 1995.

A familiar sight in the South West of England, a Sea King of 846 Sqn on a training sortie over the Dartmoor area in 1996.

In distinctive 'tiger stripe' camouflage a Sea King of 845 Sqn hooks on a light gun in Bosnia, 1996.

A gaggle of Sea King HC.4s and a solitary Mk.6CR looking for a load, RNAS Yeovilton Air Day 2007.